ARE THO ....y
in 1952. A doctor of veterinary medicine, he has also studied anthroposophic medicine, homeopathy, acupuncture, osteopathy and agriculture. Since 1981 he has run a private holistic practice in Sandefjord, Norway, for the healing of small animals and horses, as well as people. He has lectured widely, specializing in veterinary acupuncture, and has published dozens of scholarly articles. In 1984 he started to treat cancer patients, both human and animals, and this work has been the focus of much of his recent research. He is the author of *Demons and Healing* (2018), *Experiences from the Threshold and Beyond* (2019), *Spiritual Translocation*, *The Lucifer Deception* (both 2020), *Transforming Demons* (2021), *Travels on the Northern Path of Initiation* (2021) and several other books on complementary medicine published in various languages.

ENCOUNTERS WITH VIDAR

*Communications from the
Outer Etheric Realm*

From Clairvoyance to Clairaudience

Are Simeon Thoresen, DVM

TEMPLE LODGE

Dedicated to All Who Seek to Heal and Understand

Temple Lodge Publishing Ltd.
Hillside House, The Square
Forest Row, RH18 5ES

www.templelodge.com

First published in English by Temple Lodge in 2022

Originally self-published in Norwegian in an earlier version under
the title *Den Nordiske Innvielsesveien: De tre elementare Rikene Den indre
og den ytre eteriske verden Møte med Vidar og Balder # Vidar-skolen* via
CreateSpace in 2022. This edition has been heavily re-edited, enlarged
and rearranged by Temple Lodge Publishing in agreement with the
author

© Are Simeon Thoresen, DVM 2022

A CIP catalogue record for this book is available from the British
Library

ISBN 978 1 912230 99 0

Cover by Morgan Creative
Typeset by Symbiosys Technologies, Visakhapatnam, India
Printed and bound by 4Edge Ltd., Essex

Question: 'How are Christ's words of consolation received and experienced?'
Answer: 'People will feel these words of consolation as though arising in their own hearts. The experience may also seem like physical hearing.'

– Rudolf Steiner, Basel, 1 October 1911*

*From questions and answers following the lecture on 'The Etherization of the Blood' in *Esoteric Christianity and the Mission of Christian Rosenkreuz*, Rudolf Steiner Press 2000, p. 90.

Contents

Foreword   1

Vidar's Initial Teachings   3

Vidar's Latest Teachings   9

From Clairvoyance to Clairaudience   67

Methods of Supersensible Observation   73

Meeting the Vulcan, Venus and Jupiter Beings   76

Foreword

Encounters with Vidar is a continuation of my previous book, *Travels on the Northern Path of Initiation* (Temple Lodge Publishing, 2021). There, I described how, during my intense fatigue after having caught Covid-19, I traversed all three realms of the elemental world, eventually reaching what I called the 'outer realm' of the etheric. In that place – between the first elemental realm and the outer etheric world – I was met by the guardian of the threshold who introduced himself as Vidar/Balder.

The teachings I received from him were reported in the book referred to above – some added just before publication as a postscript. However, after the book had been published, the teachings continued, and almost every day I wrote down the new things that Vidar taught me. Sometimes, I simply described what had happened during the previous days, and sometimes I wrote at the same time that the conversations, visions or teachings were taking place. That is why the contents of this book may sometimes appear piecemeal and have the character of a diary. In reality, it represents ongoing research and investigation.

In the next section there is a brief resumé of the teachings previously described in *Travels...*, so that readers who haven't read that book can familiarize themselves with some of the background, as well as my initial communications, with the modern guardian of the threshold of the outer etheric world, namely Vidar.

*

With this book I am essentially inviting you to share the observations and reports of my current research. I thank you for bearing with me and for taking part, with your consciousness, in these thoughts and ideas. Many of these findings are still in the process of 'becoming'. Thus, the contents are not intended as fixed teachings, new dogmas or beliefs, but are brought forth in the spirit of open scientific exploration and discovery.

Are Thoresen
July 2022
Sandefjord, Norway

Vidar's Initial Teachings

On the threshold of the outer etheric world I met a being who introduced himself to me as 'Vidar'. At first glance, his appearance was like that of a huge, kind, childlike and smiling being, who appeared high at my right-hand side, and who, at my question of who 'he' was, described himself as Vidar – at the same time indicating that he was very close to another being, whom he referred to as 'Balder'.

I was amazed, because when I had previously travelled in the second realm of the elemental world, I had also observed the work of Vidar there, where he balanced the ahrimanic forces in material creation. In that region, Vidar was the main opponent of the ahrimanic forces – but now he appeared as the guardian of the outer etheric world, where Christ may be found.

I found it very interesting to come across him at the threshold of the higher or outer etheric realm, because the being of Vidar is also known to be the 'presenter' of Christ in the etheric world. He is described traditionally as one of the *Æsir* – the gods of the principal pantheon in the Norse religion – and the one to survive the apocalyptic events of *Ragnarok*. According to Sergei O. Prokofieff, he is the former protecting angel of Buddha.* He is also described as the angel related to Buddha's *Nirmanakaya* (the astral-etheric soul of Buddha), the keeper of the

---

*This description is found in Sergei O. Prokofieff's book: *The Cycle of the Year as a Path of Initiation Leading to an Experience of the Christ-Being*, Temple Lodge Publishing, London, 1991, pp. 263-282.

'Nathan soul' (the soul of the Nathan Jesus child, as described in the Luke gospel) and the outer and shining aura of Christ himself. Vidar also continues the work of Michael as an archangel, after Michael became elevated to the rank of an Archai.

This meeting with Vidar – and what in the way of spiritual development this brought, and may yet bring, to both me as an individual, but also to present-day humanity – was the main subject of my previous book.

Vidar and Balder seemed to be closely related. So, who is Balder? Balder is a Germanic god, associated with light, beauty, love, poetry and happiness. According to the *Gylfaginning* (the first part of the thirteenth century Prose *Edda* following the Prologue, also called *Snorri-Edda*), Balder is the son of Odin and Frigg and is married to Nanna, with whom he has a son, Forseti. Balder lives in Breiðablik, 'the place with a wide view', which also happens to be a place in Sandefjord, where I have lived my whole life. Balder had the most beautiful ship of all, the *Hringhorni*, on which he was also cremated after his death. In *Gylfaginning*, Balder is also described as being unusually handsome. Some authors indicate that Balder is the Nordic name for Christ, in which case Vidar is the outer countenance – the presenter and protector – of Balder.

In the land where Vidar was present, I was also able to meet the Christ. Up until then, I had received the light – the Godly light, the Christ Sun – with my head, with my eyes and with my third eye. To these aspects or parts of my being, the light was 'just' light, although filled with love and grace, kindness and understanding.

One morning, I tried to receive the light with my heart, and the character and presence of the light changed radically. The brightness diminished and a compassionate face appeared within it. Then I lowered my consciousness further, down to my pelvic area, and the shining light revealed a strong power – a will that seemed to be totally absent in the shining light received by the area of my head. Thus, there are three ways, or perhaps a continuum, of receiving this Christ force.

In the beginning, the teachings from Vidar were nonverbal and were instigated by an indicative look or a gesture. Amongst the things I learnt in this initial phase were:

- The importance of understanding the significant role that illusion plays in experience.
- The difference between dead thinking and living thinking. (When experiencing processes, one is in the living element, but all images of 'finished' products are dead.)
- I also had to realize that the world in which Christ lives had to be found between the two beings (Vidar and Balder), just as Christ emphasized that he would be found in the 'middle', i.e. between two or three gathered together in his name.

I then asked Vidar where I should focus my efforts, and he directed my gaze to a lump of dark soil, teaching me that it is vital that we should grow food imbued with Christ consciousness.

He also taught the following:

- The etheric forces present in earthly creation today are mainly derived from the 'inner' etheric

world. They are too strongly influenced by the
adversarial forces to be able to raise human consciousness sufficiently.

- We must draw etheric forces from the 'outer' etheric world, where the Christ light is able to penetrate.

- Rudolf Steiner could not speak openly of this
because, during his time, the outer etheric world
was not accessible to the majority of humanity, as
the three elemental realms first had to be opened.
They are now all open, but were not so until 1879,
1949 and 2019.* The key task for us today is therefore to travel through the elemental world, to
reach the threshold and gate of Vidar and Balder,
and to find the Christ light. Then, with this light,
to penetrate the Earth and its associated plant
life. Only then will we gain sufficient etheric
energy from an enlivened nutrition, enabling it
to reach a consciousness of Christ and the future
Earth condition of Jupiter.

---

*The date of 1879 is given by Rudolf Steiner as the opening to human
beings of the luciferic realm of the elemental world. The other two dates
have been discovered by myself, going back in time from the second and
the first elemental realms. These dates appear to be related to the use of
energy by human beings: the use of electricity related to 1879; the use of
atomic power related to 1949; and the current exploration of vacuum energy, starting in 2019. These dates also appear to correspond to the four
industrial revolutions, as described by the controversial author Klaus
Schwab, e.g. in an article entitled 'The Fourth Industrial Revolution'
(2016): 'The First Industrial Revolution used water and steam power to
mechanize production. The Second used electric power to create mass
production. The Third used electronics and information technology to
automate production. Now a Fourth Industrial Revolution is building
on the Third, the digital revolution that has been occurring since the
middle of the last century. It is characterized by a fusion of technologies
that is blurring the lines between the physical, digital, and biological
spheres.' https://www.weforum.org/agenda/2016/01/the-fourth-in-
dustrial-revolution-what-it-means-and-how-to-respond/

- By incorporating the etheric forces from Christ into the Earth, especially into the growing of nutritional plants, we also activate the 'Philosopher's Stone'.

Later, we will see and hear from Vidar that the threefold human being must be transformed to a fourfold one, and that this can be illustrated by the essential carbon in the Philosopher's Stone.

After these initial, nonverbal teachings, Vidar began to speak directly to me. It took some time before I managed to translate what was said into language that I could understand. After this, the first direct teachings began and I learnt the following:

- All spiritual beings usually appear in pairs; the two thus create a passage or space between them, and it is through this space that they communicate and work.
- I was shown how the weekly seven-day rhythm of time changes to incorporate a day of rest – God's rest. Time then becomes dynamic and time-cycles become asymmetrical.
- Vidar led me to understand that death is actually equivalent to spiritual life, and that the mysteries of death are incomprehensible to the adversarial forces.

Next, Vidar went into a detailed exposition that enabled me to understand and experience the whole historic development of the different earthly cultures, from the Indian post-Atlantean epoch up to the present time – and then onwards to the end of Earth evolution itself.

He explained the purpose of each culture and showed that, left to themselves, they would eventually end up in destruction. The only salvation is the Christ force (or Christ consciousness).

Vidar also taught me about the incarnation of Ahriman, which is thoroughly discussed in *Travels...*

Thus, we are brought up to date with the summary of teachings that appeared in my last book. The following chapter contains new research, which I am glad to have this opportunity to share.

Vidar's Latest Teachings

After the teaching concerning the significance and meaning of the cultural ages was completed, I was left free to travel where I wanted within the metaphysical realms. I wandered into that part of spirit-land which I have called the outer etheric world. This world was filled with cloud-like substance, although there were no clouds that hindered my view of the landscape or the beings living there. Everything was light – not unpleasant and strong, but calm and pleasant.

For a week or so, I wandered through this land. I had the sense that this was a period when I was supposed to enjoy some 'free time', like a short holiday! The entities I met were very friendly and there was no trace of the adversaries that I was so used to seeing, both on the physical Earth and in the three elemental realms. The light of Christ was everywhere, as if I was walking within an atmosphere of understanding and forgiving love. It was not a penetrating light but one of acceptance.

After a week, I turned around and entered the second elemental realm to further understand the ahrimanic forces. Then something interesting happened; I was suddenly able to regulate my height and change my measurements. I could become immensely big and infinitesimally small. I shrunk, becoming as small as an atom. I entered the atomic world, where I found that atoms did not look at all like I was taught in university.

The whole atom was actually an entity, like a spider with many legs. The legs were arranged in layers, which seemed to correspond to the seven atomic layers that I knew about. The legs had – as in real spiders – small claws on them, with which they could connect to other spiders. Their faces and eyes were very ahrimanic, on the verge of being 'satanic', or like a desert *jinn* (genie). Inside the spiders was a light – a possibility of salvation – but I felt that this was impossible without human consciousness.

This left me with some interesting considerations and questions, such as:

– Is there a correlation between the legs of a spider and so-called atomic shells?
– Are most ahrimanic beings spider-like?
– Is this world inhabited by spider-like beings because the Eighth Sphere* is the new world of Ahriman?

---

*the Eighth Sphere is the place where all ahrimanic deeds, thoughts and concepts materialize in a separate physical planet, which in the far future will be left behind by the common development of the universe and humankind. It is where deeds done without soul or consciousness will end up. It seems to me also to be a place where all our experiences with synthetic drugs, synthetic additives, pharmaceutical medicines or artificial food will take us. In addition, I believe that our work and preoccupation within the field of computer technology – machines without soul – discussions on social media, conversations through emails and all lifeless computer interactions where the soul cannot enter, will end up in the Eighth Sphere. Many occultists have spoken and written about the Eighth Sphere, but there has been much disagreement and discussion about what it is, where it is, and how it is organized. Some think it is connected to our present moon, whilst some believe it to be 'sub-earthly'. Rudolf Steiner tells us that the Eighth Sphere belongs to our physical earth. Its substance is far denser than the other mineralized substances – more so than anywhere that exists on Earth. Hence, Lucifer and Ahriman cannot dissolve it away into their world of imaginations. This sphere circles around as a globe of dense matter, solid and indestructible.

The next day, I had a hint from Vidar concerning these questions, but the hint was only that the atom actually has *eight* levels of atomic energy or individuality, as we should include the so-called centre, the kernel or nucleus. In this context, insects appear in a completely different form to spiders.

*

Over the next few days, I remained in the elemental world and shifted somewhat between the three realms, observing the differences between the beings of the third, second and first elementary worlds. In the third realm, the beings are, as described by many clairvoyants, as 'formed nature beings', both of a benign and demonic, malign nature. In the second realm, the beings are more or less like small spiders of different kinds.

The most difficult task was to observe the beings of the first elemental realm, as they are present within a vacuum, or exist in a state of 'nothing-ness'. But, if we are able *merge* into this vacuum, certain beings do become visible. They look like dark red, flowing forms… like dark-black blood streaming from the centre of the body, rather like menstrual blood. Could this be a reason why, historically, some people were so afraid of menstruation?

After a few days here, I longed for the outer etheric realm again, and turned my vision towards that world. This outer etheric world looked as described previously, like a vast wind-swept landscape filled with rivers and plains with huge mountains in the distance. This time, however, I did not just wander around as before, but walked in a straight line – a straight path towards the distant mountains. This journey reminded me a little of the book *A Pilgrims Progress* by John Bunyan (a Christian allegory written in 1678). It was also like walking over the Norwegian mountains, with their small rivers, flowers, wet areas and lakes.

The following day, Vidar elaborated a little on his relationship to Archangel Michael. He stated briefly that, even though he had inherited Michael's place as an archangel, Michael's light continued to shine over him, like from a father to a son. He was always one with Michael. Thus, in a way there is a union between Michael, Vidar and Balder.

Following this teaching, I returned to my pilgrimage towards the mountains. This took me some days, as I had no special insights or previous experiences to help me navigate. When I eventually reached the mountains, I started to climb, and I discovered that the whole mountain range was nothing but a huge black cross. The true path up the mountain was located within and inside this huge cross. This reminded me of a pilgrimage I had made some 25 years ago – and about which I have written at the end of my book *Poplar* – where I experienced a black cross with roses.*

This time, it was very different but also similar in some respects – although now seen from another perspective. I felt that my walking gave me life. The cross was alive and I climbed inside it. The whole journey brought me joy.

My experience from 25 years ago had come after I had realized that the so-called 'energetic' world is an illusion. My experience now, in the spirit land beyond the

---

* The full citation is also given in my last book, *Travels on the Northern Path of Initiation*, pp. 43-44.

threshold of Vidar, took place after I had realized that this spiritual world is actually *real*.

*

I was in Sweden giving a seminar when a friend asked me to join a group, the aim of which was to retrieve or rediscover the contents or teachings of the second and third classes of what followers of Rudolf Steiner call the School of Spiritual Science (or 'the Michael School of Spiritual Science'). This school was supposed to consist of three classes, but Rudolf Steiner died after giving the contents of the first class, consisting of 19 lessons.*

In 1924, shortly after the Christmas Conference, that had been intended to reshape and recreate the Anthroposophical Society as well as the anthroposophic spiritual movement, Rudolf Steiner embarked upon the huge task of presenting the Esoteric School founded by Archangel Michael himself. This had been originally given in the spiritual world in two sessions, first in the thirteenth century and later in the early nineteenth century. This school, that Rudolf Steiner brought down into the physical world in the form of his nineteen lessons, was supposed to be given in three classes – but after giving the first class, Rudolf Steiner became seriously ill and died (on 30 March 1925). There have been many discussions and thoughts about what the remaining two classes would contain.

To find or somehow obtain an understanding of the original contents of the two remaining classes has been something that many anthroposophists have longed for over the almost hundred years that have passed since

---

* See *Esoteric Lessons for the First Class of The School of Spiritual Science at the Goetheanum*, Volumes One to Four, Rudolf Steiner Press 2020.

Rudolf Steiner's death. This group in Sweden had the aim and goal to come into contact with such spiritual forces that could guide them to discover the contents of the remaining two classes. I was thus asked to join this group.

I asked Vidar if this was the right thing to do, and especially if this was right for me. I got a very clear and specific answer:

Firstly, that the 'missing' classes are still there, stored in the spiritual Akashic Records. Secondly, it was not by coincidence that Steiner died after giving the first class. What he gave there was, in a sense, premature, in that it was not understood by his listeners. Thus, in effect it boomeranged back on him, and was part of the cause of his death. The two further classes are as such already conceived, but they are not allowed to be revealed or published. Further, today – as so many things have changed in the spiritual world – they are not to be 'opened', or at least not yet. It would be devastating if this were to happen. Instead, the contents should be written anew, from a contemporary perspective – by people today – and thus they would be different. Lastly, this knowledge – and/or accessing this knowledge – would be especially devastating for both me and the people in this group.

Seldom had Vidar been that stern, direct and specific. This answer also explained several personal observations I had formed concerning the various people in this intended group.

*

In the old *Edda*, Vidar's foot is described as shielded or clothed with the leftover leather from human shoes. This description was important in the old Viking times, and for a long time shoe-makers threw away – as a gift to Vidar – the small pieces of material that were left over from making the toe and heal of their shoes. This documented fact has been much discussed, even in anthroposophic circles. One possible explanation for this is that people *walk* in their shoes, thereby activating will-forces in carrying out this activity. The unused pieces of leather that are cut off in the making of shoes are thus a kind of unused human willpower – a force that Vidar could use in his fight against Fenrir (the Fenris Wolf), i.e. the ahrimanic adversaries.

I then asked Vidar about this, and also if I would be allowed to look at his feet. He gave permission. His right foot was covered in a strange mass of moving and living parts, resembling a mass of roots as they appear when one has pulled up a small tree. His left foot was normal, however.

I asked him about this, and about the description from the *Edda*, which differed somewhat from what I actually saw. His answer was as follows:

> In the spiritual world, everything is in constant change, as the human soul is in constant change. One thousand years ago, the forces that bound the Vikings to the Earth were 'un-done' deeds. When they looked upon the right foot (the 'will foot') of Vidar, they 'saw' the unused leather of the shoes. Today, this is different. Today, it is the roots of trees that bind or connect human beings to the Earth. That is why the protection of trees and forests is currently engaging so many people. Today, my right foot is covered with tree roots. My right foot will always express what makes human beings venerate the

Earth, what makes them love and respect and protect the Earth – what binds them to earthly development, and stops them floating away into some kind of bliss or Nirvana. This was developed especially in the old Viking culture: the spiritual stream that flows from the north, the stream that I represent.

For several days I continued observing the figure and foot of Vidar. I also observed Balder, but he did not say or do much.

*

At the beginning of October 2021, I attended the 'Act of Consecration' service of the Christian Community church in Vidaråsen (which means, the small mountain of Vidar), in Vestfold, Norway. When the service began, Vidar became very strong and appeared as if in flames. He held the sword of Michael. The roots of his root-covered right foot became larger and looked more like ears – ears of elves. It was as if they heard everything. It seemed to me that they – or actually Vidar himself – was listening to the mourning of the Earth; to the sufferings of the elementals of all three realms of the elemental world. Indeed, it was as if he heard the sufferings of all the sentient beings of the world. It was a very impressive Act of Consecration!

*

I was reminded of the issue of the School of Spiritual Science when my Swedish friend again asked how one should relate to Rudolf Steiner's missing teachings from the second and third classes of the so-called Michael School. As we saw above, Vidar had stated that the contents should be worked out anew, from a modern perspective, to reflect the huge changes that have taken place in the spiritual world since 1924.

Now, however, something had changed in Vidar's attitude and behaviour. He seemed to open himself somehow, and a huge movement or wave rose from the region of his location and surroundings. This 'wave' contained the instructions of all three classes, but changed to fit the present challenges and constitution of the spiritual world. I had to step back to let all this information settle itself within the flow of space and time, and to enter the world or reality where I was now present. I also had to step back, because this wave was so huge and somewhat frightening.

In the beginning, this wave of information seemed to be one huge mass, but soon I discovered that it was actually composed of several layers – almost like the (three) layers of the elemental world, but also like the (nine or twelve) layers of the Earth itself – or even like the (nine or twelve) layers or sheaths of the human being. These layers were cloudy and pastel-coloured, so it was clear to me that they came out of the etheric world – the outer etheric world, the world where Vidar, Balder and Christ could be found. I sensed that it would take some time to receive this information. As the Christ entered the outer etheric world around 1933, his presence there seems to be of greater importance today than it had been at the time when Rudolf Steiner gave the initial 19 lessons in 1924.

Soon, the layers became more distinct, and separated somewhat into different colours. The first one, and closest, was green. The next one was more like red, and the farthest away was similar to blue. In the beginning, this all lacked contour and was like a formless mass. But after the following night, the lower part started to take on a certain structure. Then I realized that the more that human beings work with this knowledge of the spiritual, the more it takes on or manifests form and contours. I could see other systems of ideas and philosophies that had been given previously, appearing there like beautifully formed chests of drawers, with finely-carved oak compartments. It all was present here, in this part of the Akashic world.

Edgar Cayce described the Akasha as a library, where the librarian hands you the manuscripts at your request. As I have stated, to me these manuscripts appeared to be contained in finely-carved containers, drawers, chests or lockers. I think I could have asked for the second and third class of the Michael School, but I did not... and would probably have been denied in any case. But I did see where these contents were held: in a massive and very heavy chest of drawers, somewhat to the left of the door. In fact, it became clear that I was not supposed to ask for this information. Besides, the chest of drawers looked too huge, heavy and formal for my liking – a bit like a Greek temple. But I was determined to try to bring something new from this place – something which might be called a 'Vidar School of Spiritual Science'.

After another night of inner light but outer darkness – and presumably some sleep – this new Vidar School also took on the emerging shape of a chest of drawers, but not like the container that the contents of the Michael School were contained in. This was more Salvator Dali's 'Anthropomorphic Cabinet' (1936). It took several days for this new drawer to be 'built', as I was told that nobody had asked for this information before, and the container for this knowledge had to be made anew. But slowly it took form, and finally it was ready. I was allowed access to it, and I carefully opened the first, bottom, drawer. It contained around 50 pages. I looked carefully at them, but was unable to see any writing – although I felt that there must be *something* on the pages.

Then I carefully grasped the pages and lifted them up. Still I was unable to read what was written, and I felt a kind of despair or sadness. What if I could not read them? I lifted them a little higher, but still could read nothing. Then I lifted the pages up to the level of my eyes to see more clearly, but they then transformed into a white and sweet, sugary mixture, which seeped into my mouth. It was very sweet, and it started to fill my whole head. After this, it slowly ran down through and into my chest, where it remained for a day or two. At this point, I had no sense that any of this mixture was emerging from my body, and I no longer experienced the sensation of sweetness.

By the third day, the transformed pages had reached my diaphragm, where they again remained for a while. The process of 'seeping' through my body took about seven days, from my mouth and head region to my diaphragm, where it paused for a further few days. I observed carefully the area around my diaphragm as it lingered there. Then I became painfully aware of a strange phenomenon.

As the pages passed down by my ribs, one of them became very painful – almost like it had been broken. It was the ninth rib on my left side. After lingering at the level of my diaphragm for several days, early on the morning of 21 October, the descent of the substance continued and – totally unexpectedly and almost unbelievably – entered my 'uterus'! Here I should mention some aspects to consider when trying to understand this:

1. Rudolf Steiner clearly stated that all men have a female etheric body (as women have a male etheric body). That means that I actually have an *etheric* uterus, into which etheric pages or books from the Akashic Records could 'enter'. This was the first time that I have been able to really see and experience this female uterus.

2. In the *Kalevala*, Song 50, it is described how the lingonberry that Marjatta found in the snow entered her body and descended into her uterus, causing huge spiritual developments – the conception of a child! – to be initiated.

3. The lingering at the level of the diaphragm seems to indicate that the diaphragm might be an etheric threshold between the realm of feeling, related to the rhythmical organs of heart and lungs and the realm of will, which is related to the digestive system.

4. Having followed the Nordic Path of Initiation, which is also called the Macrocosmic Path, I now observed (with awe) that this 'outer path' suddenly changes to resemble an 'inner path'. So, it seems that these two paths may interchange or support each other.

5. It also seems that the reading of the Akashic Records or receiving a book from the 'Hall of Memory' – or even maybe from some of the higher realms of the spiritual world – needs the forces of one's will.

I watched the development of the pages in my (etheric) uterus for several days. Inside my body, the pages looked like foaming waves at sea. They were still white, but appeared to be increasingly alive, like the sea itself.

*

Three days later, the first teaching of the Vidar School appeared: not as words or mantras, but as insights or realizations. In order to understand this first teaching, we should consider some of Rudolf Steiner's statements made during his lectures on *The Fifth Gospel*. On 5 October 1913 he spoke of a communication that took place in spirit between Jesus of Nazareth and the Buddha. Buddha describes that, were humanity to follow his teachings to their conclusion, all people on Earth would live in secluded communities, as indeed did the Essenes of Jesus's time. 'But that cannot be', says Buddha: 'That was the error in my teaching. The Essenes can only progress if they separate themselves from the rest of humanity; other human souls must be there for them. The fulfilment of my teaching would result in nothing but Essenes. But that cannot be.'

Later, Jesus has the experience of seeing the beings of Lucifer and Ahriman, '...fleeing from the gates of the Essene monastery... and a question entered his soul, not as though he asked it himself, but a strong elemental force instilled in his soul the question: Where are Lucifer and Ahriman fleeing to? For he knew that the sanctity of the Essene monastery had caused them to flee. But the question remained: Where to?'

In his next lecture in the series (6 October 1913), Steiner recounts a private conversation between Jesus of Nazareth and his mother. He realizes that, through the sanctity of their lives, the Essenes caused the forces of evil (Lucifer and Ahriman) to attack ordinary people:

> 'I knew that the Essenes protect themselves by means of their way of life and their occult teachings to the extent that Lucifer and Ahriman must flee from their gates. But they send Lucifer and Ahriman to others in order to be happy themselves.' Those words greatly impressed the loving mother, and she felt herself transformed and as one with him. And Jesus of Nazareth felt as though everything that burdened him had been lifted from him by this conversation. He saw it and his mother saw it. The more he spoke, the more she heard – the more she knew of all the wisdom that had lived in him since his twelfth year. He also transplanted all his experiences into her own heart.

Thus, Jesus realizes that all the old wisdom – the old religious systems or philosophies – were no longer capable of transforming evil into good! From this, we can understand the most important awakening that Jesus had before he became the Christ. He now understood the deep significance of the 'translocation' of pathological adversarial entities – of demons – and the 'translocation' of disease. This realization now became clear and obvious to me. Steiner had described this over several pages, but had anyone come to a full recognition of its significance?

At the Baptism in the Jordan, Jesus received the ultimate solution to his question through the incarnation of the Dove, the Christ Spirit. This incorporation solved the problem of the translocation of adversarial forces or entities, namely the possibility of *transformation*. As described in my previous books,* adversarial forces and entities translocate between human beings and between humans and animals, and this is a necessity unless one can meet Christ in the etheric – because one of the main purposes of Christ is to transform evil and bring salvation to lost souls.

This phenomenon of translocation is known within most medical systems, even within anthroposophic medicine, but hitherto little has been done, in terms of education and practice, to update or modify these systems – i.e., to include a transformative model. The therapists, doctors or veterinarians working within alternative or spiritual medicine are usually not even willing to discuss this phenomenon.

The above realization was brought to me as the first of the teachings of the Vidar School. Vidar emphasized that this initiative was not a comprehensive school of the spiritual world; rather, he was concentrating on what human beings require currently in order to accommodate a modern awareness of Christ through the Northern stream. Vidar could also be seen as having the task of being the Northern face of Christ, streaming towards Europe, towards the south. The primary hinderance for this work was precisely the lack of understanding of pathological translocation, which is why this became the first teaching of his school.

*

At this point, I would like to describe how my communications with Vidar actually occur – both in terms of the

---

*See particularly *Spiritual Translocation* and *Demons and Healing*.

instruction already outlined here and as it likely applies to future such visions, teachings or communications.

A 'vision' starts with a picture, an image, that Vidar holds up in front of my 'eyes'. This picture or imagination is usually quite unexpected, and the first day I just gaze at it, not understanding very much. The vision often lasts three days, and on the second day I usually experience a sudden insight into what the image means, and also what direction the teaching might take. This has the character of an inspiration, as opposed to the first day's imagination.

Then, on the third day, it is as if Vidar speaks directly to me, explaining the whole vision and giving me a deeper insight into what he wants to say, teach and bring. This level feels like what Steiner describes as an intuition, a full understanding – almost like I am *inside* Vidar, seeing his thoughts and understanding his intentions.

In this way, every teaching consists of an imagination, an inspiration and an intuition.

*

A description of the next hindrance to be tackled – and the associated next teaching of the school – continued early on the morning of 26 October. This teaching concerns the human *mis*understanding of karma, and how karma not only affects the person in question – or those who are karmically connected to that person – but the entire Earth; indeed, the entire cosmos! This knowledge was ideally placed to be brought down from the Northern hemisphere, as it was partly incorporated previously in Norse mythology.

Vidar proceeded to show me a multifaceted prism. Then he put a small dust particle on one of the sides or facets of the prism. This grain of dust could then be seen through – or even in – all of the other facets.

Some people believe that we live in a single universe, but that this universe is one of many, a 'multiverse'. The truth of the matter is that – at least in some sense – this is right. We actually do live in such a multiverse, but it is present here and now, in its totality. In this way, we can predict or describe any of the existing multiverses by studying them. We can predict or explain this world, which we think is the only one, by studying the stellar sky, as in astrology. We can do the same by studying the clouds, water, or even a crystal sphere. When we then create karma, or change the weaving of the *Norns*,* this change can be felt or seen or experienced in all aspects of a crystal – in all of the facets of reality.

A few days later, Vidar added to this vision by showing me directly the different crystal facets relating to several of the highly esteemed people I know. They were all different, which meant to me that the insights, the knowledge, the opinions or the worldviews that these people held were actually somehow different, but not wrong. This taught me that *truth* can still be *the truth*, even if the presentation or reflection of it differs from one person to another. Still, there is only *one* truth, which is the collective totality of all the reflections, aspects or facets. The deeper we go into reality, or the higher into the spiritual world we rise, the more we see and understand the different facets or reflections, and the closer we come to the *total* truth, *the Godly truth*.

---

*The *Norns* are deities in Norse mythology responsible for shaping the course of human destinies.

During this process, I found it interesting to observe the mellow mood that I maintained, even when the influx of teachings threatened to become too big or too comprehensive for me to handle. Throughout my life, I have always felt depressed the day before I receive a spiritual revelation or understanding. Now, even though this spiritual stream was more or less continuous, I experienced a constant, mellow mood.

One other observation concerning these teachings, revelations and visions is that – as I suggested above – each one usually lasted for three days. The vision didn't initially begin with full strength, but started very gently, growing stronger and stronger until it became more alive. After one to two days, the meaning shone out brightly. Then the vision began to calm down, became increasingly still, until it gently faded away. Then, after a few hours, the next vision began.

*

The following vision, the third one, started with the growing of a red flower. It started to grow from my etheric womb, my uterus, and after a day it had filled my entire blood stream. I believe this symbolized the (etheric) transformation of the blood that human beings are now asked to perform or carry out. The blood today is filled with passions and greed, lust and egoism. The red rose or flower has no passions; it lives only in the etheric. It is now also necessary that human blood should likewise acquire such a character.

I began to ponder what Rudolf Steiner had said about the etherization of the blood. Then, after two days, the whole of the red flower started to turn brown. After three days, it had withered away.

*

The fourth vision started immediately and, after the brightness of the multifaceted crystal and the living red rose, was quite unexpected. This vision began as a lump of clay, once again in the region of my uterus. This lump of clay grew bigger and, after only one day, it had filled my belly. It became a lump of death – a sort of 'death body'. Vidar explained that, in our time, two processes are going on within our body and our being: the growing or construction of a death body, and also the growing or construction of a 'life body', a *resurrection body*.

At this point I experienced a synchronicity in the shape of a friend who stood before me at a meeting in Oslo, planting her eyes deep within mine, and asking for a discussion about the resurrection body. Following this, Vidar continued with his explanation.

In our time, there is the possibility to create two new bodies: the *resurrection body* and the *death body*. After 1933, when the possibility to experience Christ in the etheric became available to human beings, it also became possible to create a replica of the body of Christ, a so-called resurrection body, also referred to as the 'phantom body'. This resurrection body is highly spiritual and not material, although it should still be characterized as 'physical'. I understood what Vidar was referring to, as in recent years I had been working hard to understand the difference between the 'material' and 'physical'. I will not elaborate on this difference here, however.

The possibility to be able to create such a physical phantom body grew over the years, until it achieved its full potential following the total opening of the outer etheric world – and the helpful presence of Vidar – in the years around 2019. This body will be the future body of our next planetary existence, the Jupiter incarnation of the Earth. The resurrection body will be built throughout our coming incarnations, and will be kept unharmed, allowing us to add to its construction during our future lives on Earth. But – and this information from Vidar is of crucial importance – in parallel to the construction activity of the resurrection body, there takes place another construction, or rather several constructions...

After 1879, the luciferic powers achieved free access to humanity. Then, after 1949, a similar access was possible for the ahrimanic powers. And, finally, for the azuric forces around 2019. These forces are now able to build their own sensory organs inside the human being, and also their own replicas of the human organization – parallel to the already existing 'doubles' inside the human being.

Especially after 1879, the luciferic forces became able to give their form to this body. Vidar indicated this to me in the growing lump of 'clay', which he called the death body as opposed to the resurrection body. The ahrimanic forces, especially after 1949, were able to give spiritual (or actually anti-spiritual) substantiality to this death body – and this ability was highly enhanced by the entry of the azuric forces around 2019.

This body will also be physical/spiritual, but without the forces of Christ. Every time a human being thinks an anti-Christian thought – a purely material thought – the adversarial forces can snatch a small atom – the elemental spirit of the atom, of course – or fragment in order to build this death body. With this body, the adversarial forces hope to force humanity to inhabit the so-called Eighth Sphere referred to earlier – a future planetary structure totally in the hands of the ahrimanic/azuric forces, doomed for eternity (or, at least, for a very long time!) to live without the forces of the Christ.

In summary, Vidar had told me that human beings needed to be aware of:

- the translocation of the adversarial forces;
- the total interconnectedness of us all;
- the necessity of the etherization of the blood; and
- the dark plans of the adversarial forces, especially the ahrimanic and the azuric.

*

After this fourth vision, I prepared for a new one to arrive. Instead, what arose turned out *not* to be completely new. The new vision or revelation was based on the previous, fourth, one – the vision of both the death body and the resurrection body – and this enabled me to get a far more detailed understanding of both these concepts.

I saw clearly that the death body developed out of the connective tissue of the human body, especially in the abdominal area, whereas the resurrection body developed mainly from the blood circulation, especially in the heart area.

During the first day of the fifth vision – or, one may actually say the fourth day of the fourth vision – the picture of the two bodies became increasingly detailed as something of a three-dimensional structure:

- The structure of the death body gradually resembled the structure of the tendons and the connective tissues.
- The structure of the resurrection body gradually resembled the variations of warmth in the body.

*

The sixth vision developed differently to the first five visions, as it turned out to be something between a vision and a bodily experience. At first, I felt a strange activity in my head, which I felt on either side, about three to four centimetres behind each ear. This lasted for a day, after which this activity also manifested as a vision – a vision that depicted the construction of a totally new sensory organ, or rather a spiritual centre in the brain. This centre was linked to the centre of human hearing, and in some ways was related to the most important sensory aspect of Vidar himself (his hearing).

In all ages, people have experienced Vidar as a silent god – silent in his hearing. This is indicated by the leather 'ears' on his foot (as far as I could see it was his right foot) – which he explained are actually real ears. But now, ears are in development also in the region of the head and not only at the foot. What does this mean?

This new centre in the brain, behind the ears, is an important spiritual centre that is being developed now, in order to allow humanity to hear the teachings of Vidar – to hear them with our conscious mind and not only through our willing deeds. This moving of the ears from the feet, the will-pole, to the head, the thinking-pole, is a mighty sign of the times.

Is listening via the nervous system of a different quality to listening via the will system, the limb system?

*

On Sunday morning, Vidar's seventh vision or teaching began. He probably knew very well my preconceived opinion on this matter. Thus, he put forth this teaching very carefully and also in a pedagogic way. He began by showing me my 'old' viewpoint or understanding of the spiritual forces working in the human body, whereby I clearly envisioned the Christ being between Lucifer and Ahriman. Then he showed me the 'new' situation, where the beings and forces of the Azuras had also to be considered and incorporated. I thus had to accept a *fourfold* situation in the human being, with the three adversarial forces as follows: Lucifer at the top, the Azuras at the middle right, and Ahriman in the lower region. The shining light of Christ stood in the middle – in the middle of all three forces or beings.

Following this, Vidar showed me the 'old' threefold construction of the soul, consisting of the sentient soul, the intellectual soul and the consciousness soul. This is still valid, he taught, but as the resurrection body is now under development – and also, as the adversaries secretly develop the death body – a part of each of these soul properties, or constituents thereof, will be given over to either the resurrection body or the death body, and as such create a *fourth* double within the soul. This fourfolding will influence the structure of the threefold man, the threefold spiritual order as well as social threefolding (in society).*

---

*On this, Rudolf Steiner states: 'The human being of today has little feeling for the fact that every thought that is to be of value to the social life must be born out of the fundamental character of time and the place. Therefore, he does not easily come to realize how necessary it is for the Threefold Social Order to be introduced with different nuances into our present European culture, with its American appendage. If it is adopted, then the variations suited to the peoples of the different regions will come about of themselves. And besides, when the time comes, on account of the evolution of humanity, that the ideas and thoughts mentioned by me in *Towards Social Renewal* are no longer valid, others must again be found.' See

At this point, I could not fully fathom or properly understand this teaching, although for many years I had observed that more and more functions in the body are actually fourfolded (rather than threefolded). This concerned the fragments of the soul, which I experienced as consisting of thinking, feeling, will and time,* as well as the 'I' itself, which I clearly experienced as fourfold, relating to the four chambers of the heart, as described in my book *Travels on the Northern Path of Initiation* as follows:

> Concerning the heart, I can be more specific. In the heart chambers we have, in my experience, four levels of 'I' consciousness: the lower 'I', the normal 'I', the higher 'I' and the Christ 'I', which I have found to be centred in the following chambers:
>
> - The lower 'I' in the right front chamber.
> - The normal 'I' in the right main chamber.
> - The higher 'I' in the left front chamber.
> - The Christ 'I' in the left main chamber.

These mysteries required one to think and ponder further. However, presuming this vision was to 'behave' like the previous visions, there were still two days of revelations to follow...

---

lecture of 15 December 1919. Available in *Michael's Mission*, Rudolf Steiner Press 2016.

*Steiner hints at this in his lecture of 4 June 1924. See *The Festivals and Their Meaning*, Rudolf Steiner Press 2002.

Indeed, on the second day, as an attempt to help me understand better, Vidar produced several examples of where threefolding develops into fourfolding:

- Lucifer, Ahriman and Christ into Lucifer, Ahriman, Azuras and Christ.
- Hope, faith (belief) and charity (love) into hope, faith, charity and global truth.
- Freedom, equality and brotherhood into freedom, equality, brotherhood and truth.
- Nerve-activity, rhythm and metabolism into nerve, rhythm, metabolism and processes of transubstantiation (which is an offshoot from metabolism).
- Industrial system (economy), legal system and spiritual (cultural) life into industrial system, legal system, spiritual life and 'virtual' computer (digital) life (the fourth power).

In summary, it is the dawning activity of both the Archai and the Azuras that results in this double creation of a resurrection body and a death body. One creation is a Christ-life body with 'positive' transubstantiation and the other has a virtual computer life – in the form of the growing, global lies and stronger transubstantiation processes in their negative aspects.

Vidar added this as a further explanation: One hundred years ago, the world, society and the human body *was* threefold. Now, a new force has entered,* a new archangel has emerged, and forces have altered – and so now the world, the human body and society are

---

*Which many call the fourth force, the fourth industrial revolution – as we saw in the quotation from Klaus Schwab in the footnote on p. 6.

changing to become increasingly fourfold, and less threefold, in nature.

To understand that the soul forces – until now, accepted as threefold, consisting of thinking, feeling and will – also include *time*, to constitute a fourfoldness of the soul, is indeed quite difficult. We can consider that the three 'old' soul-forces, consisting of our earthly thinking, feeling and will, appear as weak shadows of cosmic forces or abilities, implanted in us as a preliminary means of enabling change to occur in the human being and the reality in which we live, both in the world and the cosmos. In which case, then *time* itself can also be considered to be a changing force, experienced in an illusory way as cause-and-effect (but in cosmic reality is a changing force).

As humans, we know that everything changes with time, and that time is the strongest changing force there is. So then, as time itself here on Earth is an illusion but in the spiritual world is a reality, thus this illusion in our soul must be a soul-force like the others (thinking, feeling and will).

Vidar also reminded me about the essential structure of carbon, which also is the Philosopher's Stone. It is fourfold. This can be seen from a diagram of a carbon molecule (below).

Personally I cannot 'defend' or explain these thoughts

– I am simply presenting what Vidar taught me. Maybe one day I will be able to fashion a proper explanation for this out of my own understanding. Indeed, as threefolding is something of a holy mantra within the anthroposophic movement, I expect to be questioned or criticized for these observations.

Here, I can speculate that perhaps the higher spiritual forces also are becoming fourfold, as in God, Christ, Holy Spirit and Sophia – thus developing in parallel to the fourfolding of society, the human body and the adversaries of Lucifer, Ahriman, Azuras and Sorath.

*

On the next and third day of this current vision, Vidar showed me that all society can be ordered according to the four principles. He pointed increasingly to the structure of the New Jerusalem, as described in the Apocalypse of St John:

> And he that talked with me had a golden reed to measure the city, and the gates thereof and the walls thereof. And the city lieth foursquare, and the length is as great as the breadth; and he measured the city with the reed: twelve thousand furlongs; the length and the breadth and the height of it are equal. And he measured the wall thereof: a hundred and forty and four cubits, according to the measure of a man, that is, of the angel.*

Vidar woke me up in the middle of the next night, and showed me that this description of a four-sided structure, like a house, was also twelvefold. He indicated this by using an example of a small farm situated quite high up towards the mountains, in a typical Norwegian valley. It looked like Gudbrandsdalen, in the area of Kvam.

Here, he pointed to a farm lying high up on the side of the valley, almost beyond the tree line, consisting of twelve houses, all of different shapes and sizes, but all with four sides (as houses usually have, of course). They

---

*Revelation 21: 15-17. King James' version.

were all made in the style of what we in Norway call *laft* (a log house built with grass on the roof). Three houses were situated towards the north, three towards the east, three towards the south and the final three towards the west. It was also very interesting to note that these twelve houses had been built according to the height mentioned in 'Revelations' (144 cubits).

After this, I could not stay in bed, but got up and wrote this all down immediately.

*

After 21 days of continuous experiences consisting of several visions, things suddenly became quiet. The spiritual world was resting, but not for long... Vidar had begun to prepare another set of teachings through visions. He began by repeating that the sole purpose of these teachings – in fact, the sole purpose of his mission – was to prepare human beings to meet the Christ; the Christ who now lingers in the etheric, and whose only desire is to enter the human mind, to enter the elemental realms of existence where human beings have their consciousness. However, to meet the Christ we also have to know his opponents, the adversarial forces.

This new vision started as a *movement* in the spiritual world, as if all the elemental beings were continuously changing place – almost like Brownian movements* seen from a microscope. As these so-called Brownian movements are not just random but follow or obey much more subtle rules than I can understand, I questioned why Vidar was showing me this.

That evening, the first vague hint appeared. The vision of the movements was intended to demonstrate

---

*Brownian motion or *pedesis* is the random motion of particles suspended in a medium (a liquid or a gas).

the azuric adversarial elementals and demons. The luciferic elementals also move in a certain pattern – a certain synchronicity, with a certain predictability. Likewise, the ahrimanic. But the azuric beings move in totally unpredictable patterns. And that is why they bestow on every single person their own personal opinions, ideas and images. As such, they foment total disagreement between all... leading eventually to the War of All against All. Everybody is totally convinced that they are right – even with regards to scientific opinions (as can be witnessed today in the public discourse over Covid-19 that largely takes place on social media and online).

*

On the second day, it became possible to see the moving 'dots' of the Brownian movements, and for the first time I was able to *envision* azuric beings in the elemental realm. I had been able to see them for a long time *inside* a human being, but not outside.

The third day brought a deeper understanding of the azuric threat, and how these beings harbour a deep hatred for all human culture. Rudolf Steiner described the Azuras as wanting illness and death for all culture, as indicated in his diagram over (although there he does not place the azuric forces as a fourth aspect as such, as the World Wide Web and internet did not exist at that time).

To me, this diagram is now a little difficult to understand, as Lucifer appears to be too dominating. But, at the time when this diagram was presented, Lucifer actually was the dominating force of the mysteries, manifesting in various functions of the third elemental realm,

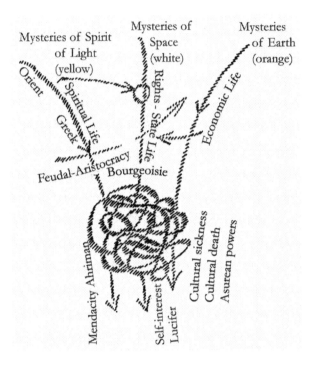

whilst the ahrimanic forces were then just an 'addition' –
waiting to be fully manifested after 1949 – and the azuric
powers were an even more external addition – waiting
to be fully manifested after 2019.

I didn't know then, but the next vision would bring
order to this somewhat complicated diagram. It began
the following day. As before, initially it was in the form
of an imagination that was initiated – once again – in
my uterus. That part of my etheric constitution began to
dominate my consciousness, and the imagination grew in
strength and measure throughout the day. I was looking
forward to understanding why the imaginations were
being born in this part of my body. I was also trying to
understand the differences between the first and second
broad round of visions.

I considered the possibility that the first round portrayed the main hindrances related to the seven cultural epochs in the fifth post-Atlantean age, whilst the following visions would relate to the seven cultural epochs in the sixth post-Atlantean age – just as it is sequenced in the revelation of St Paul. But at this point, I did not know...

*

The next day began with an insight regarding the role of the uterus – and I also experienced an astonishing synchronicity. I had been sent the sketch of one of Rudolf Steiner's blackboard drawings (see opposite), which shows three of the mysteries relating to the three adversarial forces:

- The light of the East, relating to the pitfall of the self-seeking Lucifer – but Ahriman also enters here.
- The mysteries of space, relating to Lucifer.
- And, the mysteries of the Earth, relating to the Azuras.

These mysteries were also linked by Steiner to the three functions of society, i.e.:

- Lucifer, to the spiritual (cultural) life;
- Ahriman, to the life of (political) rights;
- and the Azuras, to the economic life.

Now, Vidar showed me another way to understand these mysteries in relation to the adversaries and also the higher hierarchies. He showed me the uterus – the place of birth of many things – and he showed that this part of the body had six directions: north, west, south, east, up and down. Each of the directions were connected to a mystery:

- The north to the mystery of the Son, the Christ (which is why Vidar can and will work from the north);
- the west to the ahrimanic mystery (which is why the old sages went to America to understand this mystery);
- the south to the azuric mystery (which is why the demons of the desert, called 'Jinns', are azuric);
- the east to the luciferic mystery (which is why the eastern sages are called the Children of Lucifer, and why Lucifer himself incarnated in China 5,000 years ago);
- 'up' is related to the mystery of the Holy Spirit;
- and 'down' to the mystery of the Father (and Sophia).

All these mysteries are expressed in the *etheric* uterus. As I wrote down these lines, I still didn't understand the deeper meaning of all this, but the following day it came to me. Now it was clear:

The six mysteries express the six possible ways or paths to achieve initiation, and also to create a huge three-dimensional cross in the cosmos, indicating that all paths lead to only one being, the Christ. Also, that the two sides of the six mysteries, the male side and the female side, make twelve mysteries in total, as related to the twelve zodiacal signs, the twelve streams of etheric energy flowing towards us from the cosmos. These twelve streams form three huge crosses in the cosmos, just as on Golgotha.

*

On the morning of the third day, I *was* the cross. I experienced all twelve mysteries within myself. From my head, streaming down through my whole body, was the Nordic stream of initiation, with its three elemental realms – the stream that I knew so well. At one side, I saw the male representative, on the other side, the female, the valkyrie.*

From my feet, streaming up through my whole body, worked the Southern initiation; not so light-filled as the Northern, but with a glowing light, like that from heated iron in the blacksmith's workplace. This stream was related to the middle part of the body: the female on one side, the male on the other, in its two versions.

From the left hand streamed the Western mysteries, as the Native Americans knew them, with the great Manitou[†] flowing in, and with a deep knowledge of nature – not so different, in fact, from the Nordic peoples. Again, the female was on one side and the male on the other.

From the right hand streamed in the Eastern mysteries, and the whole wisdom of the East revealed itself in Eastern monks in deep meditation. Again, the female and the male were as two parallel streams.

From my front, streamed the mysteries of the Holy Ghost, like a huge angelic choir, singing the praises

---

*In Norse mythology, a valkyrie ('chooser of the slain') is one of a host of female figures who guide the souls of deceased Nordic soldiers in one of two paths. Half of those who die in battle go to Fólkvangr, Freyja's afterlife, whilst the other half go to God's hall, Valhalla.

†Manitou is the spiritual and fundamental life force among Algonquian groups in Native American theology.

of God, as in the European mysteries of the medieval period, revealing itself in church music with choirs.

From behind, streamed in the final mysteries, the mysteries of the adversarial powers. All the three groups of adversarial forces stood there, watching me – the ahrimanic, the luciferic and the azuric powers – saying that they, too, are necessary for the whole to exist.

Well, what could I do but make myself a cup of coffee!

*

The following day, the next vision appeared. Once again, the vision emerged from a bodily organ. This time it was the heart. My heart became alive and radiated with empathy, connecting me with everything in the world. This vision was the most personal of the series of visions relating to Vidar. I actually felt the (oft-spoken) new abilities of the heart. I felt the world and the cosmos.

My heart radiated out, much as my uterus had – although my uterus had radiated in an etheric sense. Now, my heart radiated in a *spiritual* way – a *light-filled* way, an *astral* way – reaching out to all twelve spiritual realms. Yes, there were twelve spiritual realms, nine angelic ones and the three that have been referred to as the 'Godhead'. Now, they all appeared as twelve spiritual realms – and, above that, even further depths, almost like a *new* Godhead!

In the evening, the horizontal (left–right) directions of my heart grew more prominent than the others – that is, those that come from the left and right chambers. The left heart chamber relates to the Christ, the Son, whilst the right relates to the Father. The double stream connects Christ – which represents the eleventh realm – to the fifth celestial realm. The Father – which represents the twelfth realm – relates to the tenth, the Sophia. I wondered if this was the way that Vidar was to show me the individual relations of the six/twelve directions of the heart to the twelve celestial hierarchies?

Some years ago, I had discovered that there was a close relationship between Christ and the left, main heart chamber. As I wrote in my book *Demons and Healing*:

> When making a pulse diagnosis, there are twelve layers through which we must penetrate between the skin and the centre of the heart. Most of my students stop at the fifth, sixth, seventh or eighth layers, and do not enter the heart. We need a little power to enter the heart, a little bravery, a little push.

The twelve layers of the body are as follows:

- The outer layers (first and second) relate to the astral body.
- The third and fourth layers relate to the material body: the third being our own physical, material body, and the fourth, the parasitic material body.
- The fifth to eighth layers relate to the etheric body (the four ethers); the eighth touching the pericardium and the ninth touching the endocardium, where we encounter most hindrances in therapy.
- The inner layers (ninth to twelfth) are within the heart and relate to the 'I': the lower 'I' to the ninth, the middle 'I' to the tenth, the higher 'I' to the eleventh and the cosmic

'I', the Christ consciousness, to the twelfth, where we are in the middle of the heart, the lamb (ram). We may also consider the layers within the heart as the future possibilities of human spiritual development, especially relating to the feminine part of the higher 'I's. These layers also relate to the future development of the deeper layers of the Earth itself, which today are evil but, in the future, can be transformed to good through the union of the Divine Mother and the Divine Father.

Today, I might revise the wording of this quote somewhat, but it is essentially correct.

*

The next day, this vision of the heart, with the 2 x 6 directions, was revisited. The directions from the left and right main chamber expanded further, and during the day these two chambers filled out my whole body, extending to my arms. It felt as if the purpose of these streams from the heart was to embrace the world – to embrace the *whole* world. I actually felt that I was embracing the whole world through the Christ within myself. And, that this 'inner Christ' was expressing itself through the expanded streams from both of the main heart chambers.

The other streams, though, were quite quiet during this process of expansion. Vidar told me that these other streams were intended for other periods in the history of the Earth – some had been active in the past, whilst some would be active in the future. I was told further that there are in total twelve 'calls' of the heart – calls to human beings from the spiritual world – but there are only ever two active at the same time. Was this some-how analogous to the activity of the White Lodge – the twelve high initiates known to esoteric teaching – as well as the twelve Bodhisattvas, with two active and guiding the world at any one time?

If two of them – relating to the two main chambers of the heart – were most important, who were they? Could we be talking about Rudolf Steiner, Christian Rosenk-reuz, Peter Deunov,* Scythianos,† the Master Jesus…?

Are the twelve initiates working through each of the twelve sense organs – through each of the twelve etheric streams emerging out of the cosmos through the twelve zodiacal signs – gathered in the twelve streams of the heart (as well as the other organs possibly, including the uterus)?

After this revelation, Vidar became quiet. He was quiet for some hours – indeed, for the whole day and the next day too. I thought that the teachings were over, and just waited for what would happen next.

*

The following morning, Vidar turned slowly towards Balder, presenting him as the new teacher. Balder looked at me with piercing eyes, full of strength and wisdom. Vidar's countenance had at all times been soft, loving

---

*Peter Deunov (1864–1944), was a Bulgarian philosopher and spiritual teacher who developed a form of Esoteric Christianity known as the Universal White Brotherhood.

†According to Rudolf Steiner, Scythianos is one of the highest initiates as well as the Bodhisattva of the West. He is also mentioned in the writings of some Church fathers, including Cyril of Jerusalem and Hippolytus of Rome. Scythianos is said to have been a native Scythian or Saracen who worked as a religious teacher and successful merchant in Alexandria, visiting India around 50 AD.

and mild. But Balder's countenance was strong and knowing, full of deep knowledge. He appeared darker than the lighter, traditional Nordic looks of Vidar – almost like someone from the Mediterranean.

It was obvious to me that, whilst Vidar worked through *feeling*, Balder worked through the mystery of *sight*, through the eyes. Thus, an initiation through sight or vision. In this way, the spiritual teacher Peter Deunov was connected to compassionate feeling (relating to Christ), Rudolf Steiner to 'I'-consciousness (relating to Michael), and Balder to sight or vision (relating to Scythianos).

During these considerations, my thoughts returned to what had happened a long time ago in Oslo, in the same room that Rudolf Steiner gave his famous lectures. I had taken part in a course that weekend, 30 years ago, and for some reason I had failed to arrange for a hotel room. Thus, I was given permission to spend the night on the first floor of the old house where Rudolf Steiner had given several of his lectures.

In the middle of the night I had woken and immediately sat up on the mattress on the floor where I had been lying. Two metres away, three men stood in a deep conversation. They were all dressed in black, and also wore hats on their heads. I watched them, mesmerized. They were actually discussing me! I was certain that one of the three men was Rudolf Steiner, the other was Christian Rosenkreuz, whilst the third one was unknown to me at that time. But, when many years later I saw a vision of Peter Deunov high up in the Rila mountains, I recognized him as the third person. At a certain moment, the figure on my left had turned his head and looked straight at me. Then, they all disappeared...

Now, I greeted Balder in all humility, waiting for the opportunity to get to know him better – or at least to understand what his mission might be.

Clairvoyant sight is not new to me. To a certain degree, I have experienced it my whole life – but now this clairvoyance changed its character. The whole of my surroundings became transparent – my vision could enter deeply into most objects that surrounded me, especially the elemental realms and their inhabitants. This meeting with Balder seemed to have potentized or enhanced my existing clairvoyance. Balder definitely seemed to be connected to humanity's new – or future – clairvoyance!

Towards the evening, the region on my head some centimetres behind my ears (as mentioned in a previous vision) started to stir again, this time with the character of a mild headache. This went on for at least 15 hours.

The next day, the slight unpleasantness behind my ears continued, and my clairvoyance also continued its sharpness. It was almost as if a new centre of clairvoyance had first been created by Vidar, then activated by Balder.

I reflected on what had happened previously. The three last 'activations' – of uterus, heart and brain – were at equal distances from each other, and also belonged to the three different systems of the body: the uterus to the *will*-pole, the heart to the *feeling*-pole and the area behind the ears to the *thinking*-pole. These related to the three systems of the body, as taught by Rudolf Steiner in his threefold division of human beings: the metabolic system, the rhythmic system and the nervous system. In the fourfold division of the body, there should also be a fourth part, related to time…

*

The next day, all was quiet. Likewise, the day after that. Then I realized and observed something changing. The area behind my ears – that Vidar had made me aware of – moved slowly upwards, again under the influence of Balder. After four days, it had moved about five centimetres towards the crown of my head. I followed this change with heightened awareness.

The fifth day brought a major change and understanding – but at this point the understanding was too vast to express properly. (I will, however, try to give some small hints below.) This major change was, as always, preceded by a certain depression – a certain melancholy – lasting for a couple of days. Then, the areas of movement behind my ears finally met, at the top of my head.

When this happened, I became open to time. Now I understood that my image of Vidar with huge ears does not actually indicate that he has big ears as such, but that he helps us to move the spiritual ear upwards, towards the crown (towards the chakra there?), and thus towards a certain mastery and/or understanding of time as a function of the soul, as expressed for example in memory.

Until now, Vidar had showed me aspects of time – the different cultures, the development of the Earth, for example. Earlier in my life, I had been allowed to move backwards and forwards in time. With my current insights, I could understand the extent of the help I had received to develop this ability by divine forces. I would not have been able to travel through time on my own. Now, though, given that the two 'ears' had met at the top of my head, I appeared to be able to move in time by myself – and that is an entirely different experience!

So, the fourth spiritual part of the human soul being is actually *time*, as I had suspected. But this opening up of time confused me for a while – just as, when I was five years old, I had suddenly experienced *thinking*. Likewise, at the age of 11, I was confused when I found the world of *feeling*. (I don't remember when I discovered *will*.) Now, at the age of 70, I had suddenly found and experienced *time*.

Although I believed I had known and experienced time before, I now understood that, at that time, I was being held in the gentle hands of Vidar, or other angelic beings. Now, though, with the help of Balder, I experienced time through 'growing' – towards my crown – Vidar's 'ears'.

It seems to me now that the combination of any two spiritual centres opens up the barrier of time. It might be the heart and the crown, but it might also be the ear and crown chakras (which would be three). Maybe it always takes a combination of two (or three) to open new abilities? Could that be why spiritual beings almost always appear in pairs, whether it be elementals, angels or other divine entities? Even with humans, it has to be two (or three) for the Christ to be there in their midst!

*

During the day, the two 'ears' moved even closer, resulting in an even *sharper* experience of time. With 'sharp' I mean that travelling in time felt like following a knife that 'cut' directly to the point in time where I intended to be. Not the soft or indefinite floating that I had experienced up until now, but a sharp, knife-like intensity – swift and precise!

During the sixth day, the two 'ears' moved together to the place of the crown chakra, and the described changes became even more pronounced. This new clairvoyance was, in a way, similar to the old clairvoyance that I had experienced for a number of years. But in another sense, it was very different. How can I explain this difference?

The old clairvoyance was definitely mediated through the eyes, or better described through the third eye, the glabella (the smooth part of the forehead above and between the eyebrows).

Through this clairvoyance, imaginations were the foundation – but through working with these imaginations it was possible to enter into inspiration and even intuition. Also, by special techniques, it was possible to enter time, and thus to be able to travel through time. All this was possible, and I had developed these faculties over many years.

The new clairvoyance differed from the old in the following way. (It might be possible that this faculty will change over time, of course, but this is how I experienced it now.) When going through the ears/crown chakra, it seems to me that one comes to the aspect of time as a primary point of entry. (This might be connected to time as the fourth aspect of the soul.) When I thus send my consciousness towards or into a being or object, I thus enter all the manifestations this object has experienced through all times. These experiences are still seen as imaginations, but imaginations of a different kind than those experienced when entering through the eyes. The imaginations when entering through the ear/crown clairvoyance are much sharper, more like the experience of the inner etheric realm, with its crystal water flowing in rivers and streams (think of the image of Styx).*

---

*In Greek mythology, Styx is a goddess and a river that forms the boundary between Earth and the Underworld.

This made me think of the description that Hermann Hesse gives in his novel, *Siddhartha*, about initiation. Earlier in the narrative, the protagonist possesses clairvoyance, but at a certain point in time, he embarks on the crossing of a river. There, in the middle of the river, he experiences all his former incarnations. Hesse thus connects the river, Styx, with entering the stream of time. This 'going through a river' to enter the stream of time was one of the techniques I had used earlier when entering the 'etheric stream' that flows between trees.

*

For a week or so, everything became again quiet. Then, after seven or eight days, something started to stir in the metaphysical region around Vidar and Balder. It was as if they were rearranging the props for a new scene, rather like in a theatre. This went on for a week, and increasingly I wondered what it all meant. One morning, however, I understood what Vidar and Balder were trying to tell me. Now, the teaching came from both of them.

They told me that the new clairvoyance had to be developed through Christ consciousness – as a combination of both Vidar and Balder. The new clairvoyance had to come through the face or light of Christ. Otherwise, the ahrimanic and azuric forces or beings would twist this clairvoyance, making it work to their benefit.

This above fact is something I have observed, even concerning those connected to the anthroposophic movement who have declared themselves to be clairvoyant. That their clairvoyance is real – that they themselves trust that it is genuine and real – cannot be doubted. But that it is twisted by the adversarial forces, especially the azuric forces, is also something to be considered…

Today, everything – homeopathy, acupuncture, agriculture, medicine, and even clairvoyance – has to be imbued by the Christ, otherwise it can and will be misused by the adversarial entities or forces. In olden times, this process appears to have been regulated by the good gods, the angelic hierarchies, but today it seems that we need to regulate it ourselves. We are especially responsible for this, in my view, after the year 2019.

After a week of such 'stage-setting' – and the insight I received on true and false clairvoyance – I thought that some sort of change would come, but to my great astonishment the so-called stage-setting just went on and on. Would there yet follow an addition to the previous revelations, or had I comprehended something incorrectly? Or, was some completely new revelation to be presented?

*

On Saturday morning, the second week of Advent, the teachings became clear. They concerned *time, karma* and the *Christ*. I must say that I did not fully understand the deeper aspects of the secrets revealed to me, but only the outer relationships and functions of the three aspects mentioned.

So, as time is an aspect, part or function of the soul, it changed drastically at (what Rudolf Steiner calls) the Turning Point of Time, which occurred in the year 33 AD: the death of Jesus on Golgotha and His resurrection. Christ then changed time itself, as he became the Lord of Karma. At this moment, the fourth aspect of the soul started to grow and develop, and this aspect is time/karma.

Animals do not have this concept of time – and neither do they have a concept of karma, of course! They only live within our sphere of conception of time. In our understanding of Christ, it is only we human beings who can bring these aspects or functions into the animal world, the plant world, the mineral world, the elemental world – and yes, into the worlds of the adversarial powers.

Now this teaching was complete, and the next morning the scene changed. The teachings concerning *time, karma* and the *Christ* were performed while the guardians – Vidar and Balder – were moving in a left-right direction, back and forth, for eight to nine days. They radically changed their direction of movement, coming directly towards me and piercing me with their stern, willful eyes. As before, this was of course given in an imagination, as a primary revelation or teaching. Thus it would, if following the usual path, develop into an inspiration and end up becoming an intuition.

During the next night and day, their strong gaze, their strong eyes – starting at a distance of some ten metres from me – slowly came closer and closer. After 24 hours, they stood at a distance of about a metre. This also continued during the following day, but now their eyes became softer and deeper, almost somewhat demanding and expectant...

Then, something quite unexpected happened. Vidar showed me the inner ear of a human being, with its three semi-circular canals, situated in three different directions: the anterior, the posterior and the lateral canals. And, on the inside of these three, the mighty cochlea.

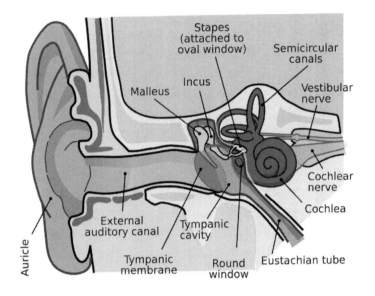

This, I was told, illustrates the close connection between Vidar and the ears, the ear chakras and also the inner anatomical structure of the ear, with its three equal canals. These represent thinking, feeling and will, with the cochlea representing time.

In my vision, all these structures started to move, to entwine, to live – and showed themselves as a model of the soul, with thinking in the vertical canal, feeling in the horizontal canal and will in the third. The time aspect is represented through the curves of the cochlea, which respond to higher frequencies as the radii become smaller, thus winding themselves into eternity.

I was studying and contemplating the cochlea that whole evening, and increasingly this study opened up to me the resemblance to time: the cochlea with its two areas of fluid, its two windows – which seemed to be very important – and its structure of membranes. I

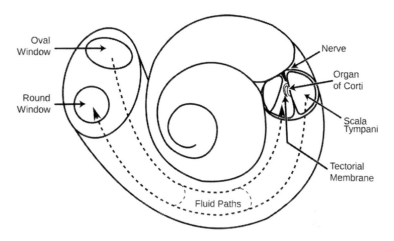

concluded that the ear is pointing to the future chakra of hearing and time. And this was very Christian in nature!

During the next two days, the vitality, size and movements of the inner-ear chakra grew both larger and stronger. The cochlea, especially, became very dominant. In the physical world, this part is firmly restricted by the hardest and densest bone in the body, called *petrous*, from the name Peter, which of course means *rock*.* This hardness of the bone points to a strong presence of the ahrimanic forces trying to limit the growth of this chakra. The ability to hear the divine word is restricted by Ahriman, expressed in this very hard bone structure. We must thus move the spiritual cochlea, and also the canals, out of the hardened area and upwards to the top of the head, towards the crown chakra.

---

*As it says in Matthew 16:18-19: 'And I also say to you that you are Peter, and on this rock I will build My church, and the gates of Hades shall not prevail against it. And I will give you the keys of the kingdom of heaven, and whatever you bind on Earth will be bound in heaven, and whatever you loose on Earth will be loosed in heaven.'

On reflection, it seems to me that both the ear chakra and spiritual hearing will be most important for the Vidar-stream. This can be sensed by the fact that within this chakra the three soul functions are separated – which is important for developing clairvoyance. Also, the fourth function dominates (the 'time-Christ-karma' part), and this aspect is restricted by the densest bone in the body, the 'Peter bone'. Vidar indicated that the development of this chakra will be very significant for the new Christ revelation.

Thus, in the future we will not strive to 'see' or 'view' Christ in the etheric world, but to *hear him in the clouds*. In the Bible, this period in time – when we can *hear* Christ in the clouds – is referred to as the culture of *Philadelphia*. Steiner referred to this as the Slavic (Russian) cultural period (approx. 3,573–5,733 AD).

In Revelation it is written thus:

> I am coming soon. Hold on to what you have, so that no one will take your crown. The one who is victorious I will make a pillar in the temple of my God. Never again will they leave it. I will write on them the name of my God and the name of the city of my God, the new Jerusalem, which is coming down out of heaven from my God; and I will also write on them my new name. *Whoever has ears, let them hear what the Spirit says to the churches.**

Note the italicized phrase, with references to 'ears' and 'hearing'. This suggests to me that we must strive to develop spiritual hearing and spiritual ears, just like those that Vidar offers us. Thus, the type of supersensible

---

* Revelation 3:11-12 (my emphasis).

perception that I have developed so far in my life – clair-voyance – now seems to be supplemented by another type of sensitive perception: *clairaudience.*

Through clairvoyance, the Nordic way led me through the three elemental realms, to the meeting with Vidar and Balder – the representatives for the new supersensi-ble sensing – which now shows itself to be based in the ear. Clairaudience is not based in the third eye, but in the cochlea – the cochlea combined with the crown chakra; or, Vidar and Balder combined. For the time being, this is what I understood of that teaching.

*

The next morning, I began to understand Vidar's and Balder's last teaching at a deeper level. This insight revealed something of an anomaly in my previous thinking, as echoed in my books, in particular *Travels on the Northern Path of Initiation.* There, I had written:

> In a lecture in Basel on 1 October 1911,* Steiner indi-cated that in the future Christ would be *felt or heard* by all that gathered to receive him. So, the adver-sarial forces will try their best, in various ways, to hinder our *clairvoyance* so that we will not be able to find the Christ.

As already quoted in the motto to this book, Rudolf Steiner had actually said: 'People will feel these words of consolation as though arising in their own hearts. The experience may also seem like physical hearing.' Thus, I became aware that Steiner had specifically said *'felt or heard'*, not *'seen'*!

---

*See lecture on 'The Etherization of the Blood', from *Esoteric Christianity and the Mission of Christian Rosenkreuz*, Rudolf Steiner Press 2000, p. 90.

During my whole life I have been clairvoyant to some degree, but not clairaudient. This realization now flowed through my body. I sat there in front of my fireplace feeling somewhat stunned.

Then, I recalled a strange communication I had had with a veterinary colleague from Berlin, after he had visited a female clairvoyant/clairaudient healer living in the Philippines. This colleague of mine suffered from terrible tinnitus, and this woman had told him: '… in your tinnitus you can *hear* Christ speaking…' Previously, I had thought that this utterance was very strange and difficult to understand. Now, however, I could feel that there was truth in it.

As I have described, I can 'enter' into any part of my body and, through this body part, in turn enter the spiritual world, keeping a certain connection to my senses or body through a silver cord. Now, I was able to do this with or through my own tinnitus, which I have suffered from for about 18 years (after driving a tractor without protecting my ears).

I 'entered' the tinnitus with my consciousness. But the tinnitus was just noise. Then I went 'deeper' – almost in the same way that I have described when I traverse the elemental realms – into or through the tinnitus. But it was still just noise. Then I went deeper, and got the impression that, through the tinnitus, I went through the third elemental realm and into the second. Still, it was just noise. Then I repeated this, and went into the first elemental realm. Still, more noise… Then I entered the outer etheric realm and listened there, carefully. Now I 'heard' something – something like words! I was amazed, but did not really understand what was being said, as I was still outside the place from which it originated.

At this point, I rested and reflected. The language that I had heard was definitely different to the language that Vidar had confronted me with when I first contacted him (as reported in *Travels...*). It seems that messages received through clairvoyance are different to those received through clairaudience – although in clairvoyance words are still 'perceived', but in a different way. It is as though clairvoyance it is more like *reading the holy script*, and in clairaudience it is more like *hearing the holy script*.

But still, I had failed to understand, so something was wrong with my methodology.

*

The following day, I did some physical work on our farm, building the new sheep-house. I needed some time to think about what I had experienced. During the work, the cochlea became more dominant in my mind. It appeared to develop and grow bigger, with greater plasticity.

The next days were both challenging and frustrating. During the previous fifty years, I had activated and directed my clairvoyance from my third eye, and this had become something of a habit for me. This led me to spiritual vision. But now, all of a sudden, I was being asked to direct clairaudience from the region of my ear, and to experience spiritual *hearing*!

I worked hard to make this change, and Vidar left me in peace to work on this for some days. My first attempt had been to stand with my consciousness directed 'forwards', and then to listen 'through' my tinnitus. This had almost succeeded, but something was missing. I then tried to turn my internal consciousness inside my head, inside my skull, by 90 degrees. I tried to 'see' through my ears. It seems strange, but something indeed began to change.

During the day, I felt as if there were two persons within myself, one directed towards the front, in the normal way, and the other directed at a 90-degree angle, to the right. It was obvious to me that there must be differences between forward-directed clairvoyance and the lateral- or sidewise-directed clairaudience.

The normal direction of human ears stands 90 degrees to the direction of the eyes. This angle can also be found in the celestial zodiac. Here, we discover that the angle between the Ahriman/Lucifer dominated axes of Gemini/Sagittarius makes a 90-degree angle with the Christ/Mary-Sophia dominated axis of Pisces/Virgo. It seems to me that the healing of this period – this time of materialism and Ahriman – is to be found in a 90-degree divergence from the dominant direction. (This must also be true for medicine, as I have described previously.)*

After a day or two, my attempt at this new method of 'hearing/seeing' expanded to include my left side, and I felt myself to be more balanced, although I still did not hear anything. Through the frontal clairvoyance, I gradually saw that the dominance of the cochlea started to diminish, although I was still in the process of understanding this. I knew I had much work to do, both with clairvoyance and with the slowly emerging clairaudience.

I worked on trying to perceive and to understand, and Vidar continued to leave me in peace and quiet.

*

---

*See for example my books *Demons and Healing* and *The Lucifer Deception*.

The following day, I came to realize what an idiot I had been! I had been trying to develop clairaudience through the ears, through the 'real' and physical cochlea. I remembered now that Vidar had already 'moved' my ears up to the crown chakra, so that the spiritual cochlea, the spiritual ears, actually lingered at the top of my head. When I tried to 'hear' through the spiritual ears, I clearly experienced a cross inside my head, between the axes of clairvoyance and clairaudience.

This cross was horizontal in nature, and something about it felt wrong. But when I moved my hearing up to the crown, the cross became a more usual, vertical (standing) cross. This felt much better. When I now tried to hear with the merged ear/crown chakra, the words that emerged were different to the inaudible words I had heard directly through my ears, even though I had gone very deeply into the source of the words.

A good picture of one's hearing ability – listening to Christ in the outer elemental world through clairaudience – is this icon (over).

Maria has all twelve ports open to the cosmos, all twelve supersensible openings through the twelve sense organs, as described by Rudolf Steiner.* This is so because this spiritual entity is totally incorruptible. The Jesus child indicates the converging of the two clairaudient abilities, merging in the crown chakra.

I set myself the task of investigating this further.

*

Following these events, I experienced a heavy cold for several days, with a headful of snuffles and pain, and

*See, for example, lecture of 20 June 1916 in *Towards Imagination*, SteinerBooks 1990.

an almost complete absence of clairvoyance or clairaudience of any kind. Then, as I emerged from illness, one morning I received the first clues as to why Vidar had showed me so definitely that Christ should primarily be *heard* and *felt* (as Rudolf Steiner had expressed it) in the outer etheric realm, rather than *seen* clairvoyantly (as I had done until now). I understood that this is due to the potential interference of the adversarial forces.

This can be explained by the direction of the adversarial forces, and the direction of the supersensible abilities of the human senses. It seems to me that the different (spiritual) senses have their directions in space, possibly related to their relationship to the cosmic streams of the zodiac. Sight is related to the Scorpion and Gemini, thus close to the adversarial forces of both the Azuras and

Ahriman – actually, in cooperation. Hearing is related to Virgo, which is the cosmic force of Maria-Sophia, to which no adversarial force is allowed to enter.

Also, the direction of sight (or vision) is frontal, the same direction as the azuric forces. The direction of the transformed hearing is upwards from the crown, which is the direction of thinking, but also of Lucifer. This force is much safer than the combination of Ahriman and Sorath (Azuras), which actually (may) bestow a false clairvoyance.

Development of clairaudience is thus much safer than the development of clairvoyance. I felt that I would just have to accept this, and continue to try to refine my clairaudience. Although I would also try to continue to refine my clairvoyance, I would need to be aware that this sense may more easily be corrupted. But maybe I couldn't use clairvoyance for a while? Maybe the transition would cause my spiritual vision to subside?

At this stage, I sent my working manuscript to a friend in Finland. His reply had astonishing consequences. He referred to a book by Valentin Tomberg, *Christ and Sophia*. Tomberg was an English follower of Rudolf Steiner, who later appeared to turn his back on his teachings and joined the Catholic Church, writing the popular esoteric studies *Meditations on the Tarot* and *Lazarus Come Forth!* However, *Christ and Sophia* was an anthology of his earlier, specifically anthroposophical writings.

The letter from my friend alerted me to several passages in the text.* Fortunately, I owned a copy, which I took from the shelf and began to study those pages.

Christ and Sophia, Anthroposophic Meditations, SteinerBooks 2006, pp. 259-260, 263-264, 272.

What I discovered there shocked me. Valentin Tomberg described exactly what I was experiencing. For example, he states that the directions of human thought are two-fold, one spreading out horizontally, with the character of the sense of sight, and one directed upwards, first experienced as a kind of hearing or listening to the Word from above. From a moral perspective, the horizontal thought stream represents one's own thinking in active apprehension of the world from within the 'I', whereas the vertical current expresses a devotional attitude to the world where truth originates.

According to Tomberg, two types of human being, with different spiritual organizations, appear after the Mystery of Golgotha. One type is 'blind' but has developed the capacity for hearing the spiritual word, and one type has 'sight' but is 'deaf' to the spiritual worlds. These two groups rely upon one another, so that the 'eye witnesses' and 'ministers of the word' collaborate to comprehend the Christ event.

'Ministers of the Word' make knowledge of the Christ possible to the 'eye witnesses' because only hearing the voice of Christ in a purely moral way gave direction to the vision of those who 'saw'. The faculty of believing without having seen is the capacity to hear and recognize through the ascending thought capacity in the front of the human head. The forehead has a deep connection to the zodiacal sign of the Ram. Indeed the subjective horizontal thinking was named 'Ram' because of the associated subjective horn activity, whereas the vertical thinking was named 'sheep' and is related to hearing, obeying the higher worlds, and is not subjective, thus producing no 'horn' formation. This points to those specially organized to receive the Christ Impulse by being able to distinguish the voice of the 'Good Shepherd' from the voices of Lucifer and Ahriman.

The effect of the Christ Impulse on spiritual sight and hearing is expressed karmically by the fact that those who possessed spiritual sight in anticipation of Christianity had to lose it, in order to develop moral and spiritual hearing (the 'voice of the shepherd'). Hearing the voice of the shepherd is essential for a conscious acceptance of the Christ Impulse. Therefore, in order to consciously receive the Christ Impulse, those who 'saw' had to undergo a reorganization that would make them dependent for a while on the vertical current of 'hearing', whereas those who were already 'blind' when they encountered the Christ Impulse (who received it through hearing the voice), I received their 'sight'.

Activities of human beings today reach no further than the 'feet' of the higher human being or 'head' human. These 'feet' are located in the hearing organism and the effect of cleansing the 'feet' as a rule only reaches as far as the human ears. In rare cases it might reach to the 'feet' of the 'thorax' human in the centre of the body, and the feet of the lower human being (the real feet) will not feel the effect until the sixth cultural epoch. In the present age the task of 'foot washing' is limited by the injunction 'He that hath ears to hear, let him hear' (Mark 4:9).

There is much more of relevance that can be studied, but the above is a summary of some of the more pertinent passages. These now convinced me of the need for humanity to develop clairaudience in addition to – or at least parallel to – clairvoyance. Otherwise, we will not be able to protect ourselves from the 'twisting' activities of the adversarial forces. Unfortunately, as I have previously described, I have seen such twisting in too many good persons who believe they are serving the good.

At this point, my intention was to end this book, and I even wrote a rather depressing conclusion, feeling that aspects of my life's work may also have been twisted or corrupted by the adversarial forces. But Vidar cut through my dark mood, asking me to develop the above themes further. I was to elucidate the necessary development from clairvoyance to clairaudience. I was glad to attempt this.

From Clairvoyance to Clairaudience

I have experienced and developed clairvoyance throughout my whole life. Through my training in pulse-diagno-
sis, I developed clairsentience, analyzing patients' pulses
many thousands of times – either directly through treating humans or indirectly by using my own pulse when
treating horses, dogs and cats. Now I am beginning to
appreciate more fully how clairvoyance can be misused
or corrupted by the adversarial forces – especially since
2019, when the azuric entities have been able to enter the
human organism. There, they inspire lies, but also provide a hiding place for the ahrimanic entities, who want
to induce a corrupted and false clairvoyance in human
beings.

Whether clairsentience can be easily misused, I am
not yet sure, but as this system originated in the court of
the Yellow Emperor (Lucifer),* I suspect that it can. Nevertheless, as we have seen, my communications with
Vidar have led me on a path to developing clairaudience, and I have understood the necessity of attempt-
ing to do this. I will continue by describing my further
efforts along this path.

*

A headache lingered at the top of my head for a long
time. It had started around the beginning of December
2021, in connection with a common cold – but after the
cold was over, the headache did not go away. It actually

---

*See further in my book *The Lucifer Deception*.

got worse over the following days, causing worry and exhaustion. Eventually, though, the headache vanished, and I was able to observe a peculiar development.

I had always experienced or felt my clairvoyance around my physical eyes, possibly very close to the so-called 'third eye'. This experience of my clairvoyant ability now slowly moved further into my brain, towards the pineal gland – in fact, towards a central line between my two ears.

When my clairvoyance reached this line, the path it followed turned upwards. It seemed that the clairvoyant third eye might eventually join with both of the two clairaudient ears, in the region of the crown chakra. I do not yet know for sure if this will happen, but it seems a possible (or likely) conclusion of this long process.

Then, something unexpected happened (as often it does during travels – both in this world and in the spiritual). The movement of my ears towards the crown, as well as the movement of my third eye further back in my head and upwards, had always felt as though they were following a line – a very thin path. This structure had no content, no function, other than a path. I felt a certain sorrow in this movement, as it seemed to be changing something that was both dear to me and that also felt secure.

I had not reckoned with the mystery of Christmas, with the coming of the Saviour to Earth. On waking at around 7.30 am on the morning of 25 December, on Christmas day, the structure of the ascending line from the centre of my brain, the junction between the horizontal 'clairvoyant' ability and the ascending 'clairaudient' ability, radically changed. It became like a hollow tube, like a trumpet, with the wider part reaching upwards.

This change was not an illusion. It lasted, it was stable, and the trumpet became clearer and clearer – even somewhat wider as time progressed. This change gave me hope for a coming clairaudience.

During the next two days, the 'trumpet' changed somewhat, becoming bigger and wider. Also, the horn became alive, like the mouth of a coral. At this stage, I cannot do other than make a parallel to the Revelation of St John. After the seven congregations are addressed – which represent the time-periods of this cycle – the seals are broken – which are the time periods of the coming cycle; but also, in my interpretation the opening of the seven supersensory sense organs.

The trumpets are heard – which point to the seven time periods of the last great time cycle, but also the activation of the seven supersensible sense organs. Vidar is now revealing or describing the first of these seven trumpets, the one related to the hearing of the Word – of the Christ – through clairaudience, obtained by the three streams of the senses: two from the ears and one from the eyes, meeting at the top of the head.

All this that is described is obviously my personal interpretation and experience of the coming times, as well as the necessity of the present time. However, according to my reading of Valentin Tomberg, as we saw in the last chapter, the above is the development of the two 'eyes', one which is the third eye, that opens for clairvoyance, and the other is the eye-ear-crown eye, that opens for clairaudience. Or, one may say, the hearing/seeing of the cosmic Christ-Word. It is the harmonizing of the two eyes; the upper eye sees the mysteries of goodness, the future and the world of spirit, while the lower eye perceives the mysteries of evil. And the line between the two eyes is the Trumpet of Intuition of the future.

Rudolf Steiner describes this a little differently in a lecture about the reading of the pictures of the Apocalypse:*

> After the seer has perceived the spiritual beings in the astral light for a while, they begin to sound forth. This is described in the resounding of the trumpets when the sixth seal is opened. That is the condition of Devachan. The seer becomes 'clairaudient', able to hear spiritual sounds – the spiritual ear is opened.

Let me underline or clarify that in my interpretation it is not the spiritual ear as such, but a combination of the eyes and the ears which move or merge with the crown chakra. Or, at least it was so for me.

Over the following days, the 'trumpet' increasingly became alive. Whereas previously only the horn part of the trumpet – resembling a mollusc – had been organically alive, now the whole instrument was so. It began to resemble a fallopian tube, moving and working inside my brain. The upper part, the opening, was at the crown chakra, whilst the lower part stretched further and further down, reaching the upper part of the throat (the pharynx).

At this stage, I started to hear something like thunder, deep within the cosmos. I observed this as taking place in total darkness, although a 'warm' sort of darkness— something like being inside a living being.

My initial experiences with clairvoyance always took place within some kind of light. This time, as I have

---

*Reading the Pictures of the Apocalypse, SteinerBooks 1993, lecture of 1 May 1907.

indicated, I experienced it as a *warm and living* darkness, almost like a foetus experiencing warmth and sound inside its mother. This experience made me feel as if there was a foetus inside my head, waiting to be born!

In the beginning, this tube – somewhat like a hearing aid – acted in something of a childlike, lively and undifferentiated way. But after a day or two, it became much more mature, less pliable and differentiated. It did not reach further than the upper part of my vocal cords or the region of the pharynx.

Every time I tried to listen through this 'hearing aid', the air was filled with distant thunder, distant rumbling. When I tried to 'see' through this tube, an image arose of dark stones featuring letters that emitted light – a golden light. I still did not understand either the thunder or these letters.

Thus it went on for several days, and all the time the tube became more and more 'physical', increasingly structured. It had started off as something very etheric in nature, with almost no structure. Then it developed to become hardened and more structured – and eventually the etheric element appeared to transform into part of the physical structure of my brain.

*

One aspect of reality that has been revealed to me from this new way of spiritual observation is that the spiritual world is different according to whether it is experienced through clairvoyance or clairaudience. To clairvoyance, creation and the spiritual world is illumined and made visible with the help of light, whether it be the strong light of Lucifer or the more subtle light of Christ – or possibly other kinds of light revealing or connected to other spiritual beings, either of a beneficial or malevolent nature.

Through clairaudience of the combined ears-eyes-crown chakra, the spiritual world is not lit up or made visible by the help of 'light' of any form. It is made visible by the help of sounds, initially heard as thunder. Later, through the image of dark stones inscribed by golden letters, it is made visible through the power of *gold*.

These were the experiences bestowed on me through my new abilities during the days of the Twelve Holy Nights between 2021 and 2022.

Methods of Supersensible Observation

At this stage in our deliberations, let us take a step back and recap. We began this book with teachings from the Vidar School, focusing, at a certain point, on the future development of clairaudience. As we have seen, clairvoyance has the danger of the intervention of luciferic forces. In clairvoyance, one always 'saw' the images in light, but in clairaudience one received all information in a warm darkness. (In some legends, it is said that Lucifer took the light in the beginning, whilst Christ was left with the darkness.)

According to my communications with Vidar, the best and safest method to receive spiritual information today is clairaudience. I have described how Vidar instructed us to develop our supersensible organ of hearing, and in the last chapter we saw how this supersensible organ of hearing is developed. I will describe further how that work continued, and my experiences with this special kind of supersensible receiving.

Here, as something of an interlude, we will describe several methods of supersensible observation, as well as several 'organs' through which such observation is possible. The adversarial forces and entities have also created or built their own versions of the sense organs, so that it is possible to mistake a genuine supersensible observation with one that is coloured or influenced by the beings of Lucifer, Ahriman or the Azuras.

The senses described by Steiner are extremely complex formations, as they exhibit both an outward and an inward direction of flow. For example, the eyes that perceive the cosmos send an outward etheric stream, enabling them also to receive an inward flow of information from the object that they are viewing. It is a general spiritual rule that any movement automatically creates a counter-movement, and this is even relevant for 'time'.

The twelve senses are also developed in the luciferic, ahrimanic, azuric and human karmic doppelgängers. These four entities employ the senses in a unique way. The human karmic doppelgänger uses the physical sense organs as we use them in the material world. The ahrimanic, azuric and luciferic doppelgängers, however, create their own mirror images of these structures. The templates that ahrimanic and azuric forces utilize are situated deeper within the physical body, whilst the luciferic templates are more superficial, infiltrating the astral sheath. For example, in the eye the ahrimanic sense organ lies about 1 cm behind the material optic structure, whilst the luciferic is in front of the eye. I perceive the ahrimanic structure with my clairvoyant ability as greyish, similar to a tin plate.

These structures are also activated and developed by viewing electronic screens. From this information, it can be surmised that there are actually three aspects of each of these sense organs. If one considers all twelve sense organs and combines the fact that each of these senses are employed by three doppelgängers (including ourselves), and that each organ is involved in both an outgoing and an ingoing stream, we can conclude that we are actually dealing with 72 qualities in total that should be considered when understanding sensory and supersensory experiences! Note that all twelve senses can observe spiritually. If the spiritual eye is developed, for example, we refer to its ability as clairvoyance.

Finally, to observe the spiritual world through any of the supersensory sense organs without the transformation of thinking – actually also the transformation of feeling and will too – will lead to error.

Meeting the Vulcan, Venus and Jupiter Beings

Following the experiences of the Holy Nights, I returned to my meditative work with new vigour. I had been waiting for almost two months for the 'trumpet' to begin functioning as a supersensible sense organ. Now, in the new year, this new faculty started to show some kind of activity, i.e. it was beginning to resemble a sensory organ...

At this time, I received an interesting question from an American friend, asking me to query Vidar regarding the 'Vulcan beings'. Rudolf Steiner had spoken about these entities as follows:

> The beings I have spoken about will descend gradually to the Earth. Vulcan beings, Vulcan supermen, Venus supermen, Mercury supermen, Sun supermen, and so on will unite themselves with Earth existence. Yet, if human beings persist in their opposition to them, this Earth existence will pass over into chaos in the course of the next few thousand years.*

To put this question about these mysterious Vulcan beings, I had first to use my clairvoyant ability to make myself 'stand' directly in front of Vidar. Initially, that first day, he simply did not react. Then, on the second day, he showed me five or six individual entities. He indicated that there were many types of beings coming to Earth to

---

*Lecture of 13 May 1921 (GA 204), *Materialism and the Task of Anthroposophy*, Anthroposophic Press 1987.

help us, but as I had asked specifically about the Vulcan beings, he would show them to me – or rather, put me in contact with them.

And there they were. They were greyish, about 150 cm high, with pointy ears and a long 'cloak' or mantle. They also had some kind of cloth around their heads. They resembled old and impoverished human beings. I tried to attract their attention, but in vain. They seemed to be motionless and with a single expression on their faces: a sort of unresponsive dullness.

The following day, something changed in their feet. And, after another day, their hands too. They started to indicate their feet and hands – and, in showing me, their mood lightened, becoming good-humoured and jolly. Now I could see that in both the soles of their feet and the palms of their hands were *eyes*! There was one relatively large eye socket in each of their soles and palms, i.e. four in all. After they had shown me all this, they seemed to become more lively, and they even moved rhythmically, using something like dance-steps… Maybe they were happy they had contacted a human being?

I awaited further contact and communication.

*

The following day, the communications began to flow more freely, and I received the following messages. Firstly, though, the Vulcan beings presented me to their friends and co-workers, the Saturn beings, the Jupiter beings, the Mars beings and also – but to a lesser degree and somewhat more hidden – the beings from Mercury, Venus and the Moon. They all stood there in front of me, in shining clothes, rather like medieval armour. They all were in different colours, but the Mars beings were the brightest, with deep-red armour or dress.

Then, in very clear concepts, the Vulcans told me what their mission was: to make human beings be able to see the *life* of the planet – the life of trees, animals and nature. When human beings are able to feel the real life in all living things – the etheric, astral and spiritual life in all creatures with which we coexist, we will behave and act differently with the world. This emergence into nature comes about through the mastery of the will, expressed in the 'will' of the hands and the feet. Opening to the totality of life will also include the three elemental realms – as well as the angelic hierarchies – and thus enable us to work spiritually into all these realms in a (white) magical sense, in full consciousness and with a loving attitude.

In this way, these beings were helping Vidar and Balder. Vidar, with his ears on his foot, is 'hearing' the Earth. Balder is bestowing the new clairvoyance and clairaudience, whilst the multitude of planetary beings, including the Vulcan beings, are opening our 'will-eyes' to the Earth, nature and the universe. This activity brings human beings to a living connection with *all* life.

When I reported these experiences back to my friend, he sent me several additional – and somewhat technical – questions, as follows:

- How do we work harmoniously with all of these beings? What relationship should we have with each of them?
- In coming to know life processes, how do we prevent the temptation to use them (e.g., the cow's digestive rhythms) in 'mechanical occultism'?*

*See *Harmony of the Creative Word*, Rudolf Steiner Press 2001, Lecture 2.

- How can we move forward towards attaining the goal of the *interpenetration* of the moral and the mechanical?
  - What role will this interpenetration have for those on the human stage of Jupiter?
    Will this interpenetration be akin to the interpenetration of light and dark (giving us colours)?
- A moral impulse must begin with the 'I-Am' which moves the astral that vibrates the etheric body.
  - How can we distinguish the moral vibration of the I-Am from an immoral one, or from an impulse arriving from the astral?
  - What materials-apparatus will detect a moral impulse within a mechanical device?
- What is the right concept for electricity that can enable it to take its proper role in evolution?

It is important to understand that our helpers, Vidar, Balder and the different beings from the old planetary realms, are here to help us experience the spiritual world, and not primarily to give us detailed answers to all our questions. I kept these somewhat specialized questions in the back of my head, but felt that their answers had to be sought for individually.

But then there occurred something of a synchronicity – or even a karmic response? Just two days after receiving this list of questions, I ventured on a journey to Devon in England, to give some lectures and workshops on the teachings of Vidar. From there I travelled to the Alhambra in Granada, southern Spain, where I continued to teach. This work began to provide pointers or inklings of answers to some of the above questions. As I say, it is for us to work and to win spiritual insight. Nevertheless, conscious striving in life will always provide glimpses of truth...

*

I will begin by describing something of my travels to the United Kingdom and Spain. The journey to Totnes, Devon, was quite exhausting: two hours by train to Oslo, two hours of waiting at the airport, two hours flying to London Heathrow and then six hours of being driven to the market town of Buckfastleigh near Totnes. On the journey, we passed close to Stonehenge and the town of Amesbury in Wiltshire. The adversarial darkness surrounding the mysterious artificial mound of Silbury Hill was thick and opaque, but as we journeyed closer to Totnes, spiritual lightness filled the atmosphere, becoming stronger than the darkness.

According to Geoffrey of Monmouth, 'the coast of Totnes' was where Brutus of Troy, the mythical founder of Britain, first came ashore. This brought my thoughts to a very interesting geographical discovery I had made some years before, when investigating the three major initiation centres of the *Dróttinn* culture (a culture that, in my view, preceded the Druid culture).

There are/were three major centres of this Dróttinn culture:

- The north-east centre, on the Solovetsky islands in the White Sea, situated north-west of Russia.
- The 'middle' centre, in the region of Skiringssal in Norway – an area where I grew up.
- The western centre, situated close to Totnes in Cornwall.

One of the main peculiarities of the Dróttinn initiation was the Troy maze or labyrinth. I will say something more about the Troy maze, as I had previously linked the area around Totnes to the Trojans, long before I visited it. Now I learned (to my great amazement) that Totnes actually was, supposedly, founded by refugees from Troy!

Several labyrinths, like the ones we find on the Solovetsky islands and also near Skiringssal, are known in Europe from olden times, but especially in Scandinavia. From ancient times, these constructions have been called Labyrinths of Troy. Variations of this name – such as Trøyenborg, Trøborg, Trelleborg, Troytown – are found all over Europe. The origin of the name lies in the mighty old city of Troy.

Why this name is connected with the labyrinths is uncertain, but we may discover some relationships if we investigate the ancient city culture of Troy. Homer's *Iliad* describes in detail the fierce war between Sparta and Troy. At that time, Troy was the most western outpost of Eastern philosophy and thinking, while Sparta was more Western-orientated. Troy had captured and imprisoned Helen, the beautiful princess of Sparta. After several years of fighting, Helen's followers set her free. They managed to conquer Troy by the help of a giant hollow wooden horse (the Trojan horse), in the belly of which hid many soldiers. We could say that, via this wooden horse, the Western way of thinking gained access to Eastern philosophy. The constructors of the Troy castles were possibly Oriental horse-warriors who rode from the East during the time of population migrations, settling in different parts of Europe, especially Scandinavia. (I would point readers who would like further information about Troy castles to my book *Transforming Demons*.)*

*pp. 7-9.

If we walk the paths of the labyrinth, we start in the middle layer. After that, we move outwards in two turns. We head inwards in two turns almost to the centre, outwards again two turns, and finally towards the absolute centre. The correlation of the labyrinth with Asian teachings concerning the paths or construction of the Qi flow in the body and the claimed effects in 'walking' or 'thinking' these paths is not absolute, but is amazingly coherent. These imaginations or beliefs are consistent with the beliefs of our Scandinavian forefathers who were occupied with fishing and hunting. The only difference is that our forefathers travelled physically, whereas the Asian shamans did the exercise mentally. (It is uncertain if this knowledge was universal at the time or was discovered by our European forefathers, or if Asian horse-warriors brought them during the times of the population migrations. However, I would argue that the last possibility is most probable.)

The three main Dróttinn centres of initiation lie on a straight line, going from Solovetsky in the north-east to Totnes/Tintagel in the south-west. On this line between the three mystery centres, we can also link the lectures Steiner gave in the western sphere of England, in the middle sphere of southern Norway and in Helsinki. All these lectures concern the kinds of forces that are in these three places, the kinds of initiation that are possible there, and also the kinds of occultism it is possible to develop.

Thus, one could associate the three occultisms with places as follows:

1. Totnes with the development of mechanical occultism
2. Skiringssal with the development of hygienic occultism
3. Solovetsky with the development of eugenic occultism.*

*

Back on my travels, we arrived in the light spiritual atmosphere of Totnes, more specifically in nearby Buck-fastleigh. It was as if the secrets of the second elemental realm were openly visible in this region. I could even observe the different 'atoms' and 'molecules'. (I am well

---

*The reader can find more about the meaning of these 'occultisms' in Rudolf Steiner's *Challenge of the Times*, Anthroposophic Press 1979. I also discuss their meaning and quote extensively from the aforementioned book in my *Travels on the Northern Path of Initiation*.

aware that atoms and molecules are an illusion – *maya* – and that they are in fact the reflection of the elemental beings that are their foundation, but I use these names for people to understand.)

When I 'opened' these different atoms or molecules, a clear sound was heard, as if Christ was inserted in the middle of each one, causing a vibration. According to my research, the various atoms have their own frequency – their own sound – which make some 115 different vibrations. It seems to me that only the presence of the Christ in 'the middle' can create this vibration – and thus that only a moral presence can activate this frequency.

The insertion of Christ in an O atom, or an O_2 molecule, created a vibration close to G. The activation of CO_2 created a vibration close to A. When I thus inserted Christ in the middle of O_2, many of the participants of the seminar felt that the air had become more fresh, and it became easier to breathe.

From Totnes, we travelled to Stroud, where I was teaching at a gathering of biodynamic farmers. We were to discuss the Christianizing of the elemental beings. From Stroud I flew on to Malaga, and then travelled to the great Moorish palace of the Alhambra in Granada.

Being confronted with the Arabic art in and around the Alhambra was like a continuation of my experiences in Totnes – almost as if it had been planned to be so. The Arabic art was definitely inspired by the second elemental realm, just like the spiritual atmosphere in Totnes, and it suddenly became obvious to me that this was the deeper reason why both the Alhambra – and, hundreds of years previously, Gondeshapur* – had to be cleansed from Arabic culture. This had to occur before the second realm opened in 1949, when Christ could be found there. If this realm (as well as the first, which opened in 2019) was opened before Christ could be found and experienced in the outer etheric world, Ahriman and the Azuras (Sorath) would be able to conquer these realms, with catastrophic consequences to humankind.

Without the presence of Christ, we cannot win the fight against the adversarial forces – waged since 1879 – over the astral body; the fight over the etheric body, waged since 1949; and the fight over the 'I', starting in 2019. The adversarial forces wanted this fight to start prematurely, so they could gain the upper hand. They would not have been able to achieve this if we had Christ on our side.

Then, in the early seventh century, Islam was introduced to the world through the prophet Muhammed. This impulse put an end to the development of the science of the second elemental realm in Gundeshapur, where – according to Paul Emberson in his three-volume work *From Gondishapur to Silicon Valley* – the intellectual and spiritual foundations of the computer were to be laid. In the same way, the influence of Arabism had to be stopped in Spain, and eventually the Moors were defeated, converted, destroyed or thrown out in the centuries leading up to 1492 AD.

Today, we are able to penetrate into the first elemental realm, where we must face the azuric beings, for which we must acquire the help of the Christ. The azuric beings

---

*Gundeshapur was the intellectual centre of the Sassanid Empire and the home of the Academy of Gundishapur, founded by the Sassanid king Shapur I. It was home to a teaching hospital and had a library and a centre of higher learning.

adhere to our body, just under the heart and slightly to
the right side. This is also the area where the new heart
chakra, the Christ chakra, will develop. We thus see
that the development of Christ and the Azuras are quite
closely connected.

Another revelation about the Azuras came to me the
day we left Alhambra. Then, the air was thick with red
dust from a huge sandstorm in the Sahara. This storm
also brought with it a number of elemental beings from
the desert. As I had encountered such beings before, I
immediately recognized them as azuric elementals. They
are destructive as the dust itself, destroying machines
and technology. This indicates a parallel to the demonic
elementals created by solar panels. They are created
where the sunlight is captured by the silica molecules
and transformed to electricity. In the desert, the sunlight
is absorbed by the pure sand, which is silica, and azuric
elementals are created from this.

Another observation concerning the influx of azuric
elementals into Europe concerns the Sirocco winds from
northern Africa. People's psyches change when such
warm winds penetrate into Europe. At the Hebrew University in Jerusalem, pharmacologist Felix Sulman has
been studying physiological responses to Israel's version of the Sirocco. He finds that almost one third of the
population experience some kind of adverse reaction
to the Sharav winds, and of these 43 per cent show an
unusually high concentration of serotonin in their urine.
This is a powerful and versatile hormone that causes
the constriction of peripheral blood vessels – including
those in the brain – controls sleep, and is responsible for
the development of mood. It is a natural tranquilizer,
but too much of it produces clinical symptoms which

include migraines, allergic reactions, flushes, palpitation, irritability, sleeplessness and nausea. These effects are definitely related to the blood system, and as such to azuric elementals.

*

Back home, I rested for a while before Vidar's teachings continued. On the morning of 23 March, I experienced something of a breakthrough. As I mentioned, I had asked Vidar how human beings could relate to the Vulcan beings. I had already had the experiences mentioned, but I had remained largely passive during these processes, just receiving the images and messages. On this particular morning, however, I realized that I had to speak to the Vulcan beings directly – and then everything changed.

I addressed one of the beings, who somehow appeared to be a leader. This conversation developed in much the same way as my conversation with the 'hidden people' or elves of Iceland. (They had told me how closely they were attached to humanity, and that the spiritualization – that is the Christianization – of humanity was the only thing that could liberate them, as they were created in connection—almost as 'mirror beings'—with human beings.) The Vulcans, however, presented their own creation story. They were not mirror beings of humans, but were still connected with human development, or at least Earth development.

The Vulcans were human beings on Old Saturn, the stage of development when humans laid the foundation of their 'I', as well as their physical body. There, they (or at least a certain part or group of them) stayed behind, as a reflection or a mirror action of the azuric beings that were in the process of development or creation at the same time, and who also stayed behind at the same stage.

The future destiny of these Vulcan beings was to incarnate in the same period as the azuric realm opened to human consciousness. This was in order to help human beings survive the opening of the azuric realm – the first elemental realm, that opened fully in 2019 (which also has a close relationship to the Covid-19 pandemic).

Any remaining fatigue from my travels now disappeared. Conversing with the Vulcan leader was invigorating! He explained, further, that the Vulcans, being voluntary laggards from Old Saturn, expected to fulfil their mission on the future Vulcan incarnation of the Earth. The Venus beings came from Old Sun, and were meant to fulfil their development on the future Venus incarnation of the Earth. They were using the Earth as a halfway stop. The Jupiter beings were laggards from Old Moon, and were intended to fulfil their development on the future Jupiter incarnation of the Earth, and were also using the Earth as a halfway stop on their current path.

Their current mission is to help us in our struggle with the adversarial forces and hordes: the Vulcans to help against the azuric beings, the Venus beings against the ahrimanic hordes and the Jupiter beings against the luciferic. As voluntary laggards, they themselves need this Earth development to properly evolve. Their work here to is to help in transforming the aforementioned adversarial forces, enabling them to incarnate in the future stages of Earth development as positive forces or spirits.

The Vulcan, Jupiter and Venus beings are ready to enter the three elemental realms, together with the Christ, but humans have to open these realms for them, leading them into the elemental world. Then they can help us – by being seen and acknowledged – simply by their presence. These were the teachings of the Vulcan elder.

After this, the Vulcans, as well as the Jupiter and Venus beings, became quiet for a few weeks. I contacted them every day, asking for a conversation, but they showed no interest or emotion.

*

After a period, there was once again life within the group of celestial beings. The Vulcan, Venus and Jupiter entities all started to move. They also started to look at me. As I have previously described, this slow change in contact with spiritual beings is quite usual. I simply needed to be patient.

Now the celestial beings saw me, observed me, whilst again they moved in a sort of dance – a dance without any system, as far as I could see. This lasted for several days, as they became increasingly aware of my presence – although clearly they didn't want to communicate with me directly. However, the dance become more and more like a 'real' dance, which meant that I started to see a system within it, a kind of logic in their movements.

Then, the week before Easter, the cosmic beings came closer to me, just a few inches away from my face. This could have been unpleasant, but I consciously accepted their closeness. I asked Vidar if all was fine, and he nodded. I accepted the closeness of the beings, and they were allowed to 'enter' me. They then started to do this – first in the area of my face and head. In this 'entering', they approached in a formation of three, that is, all three types of entity approached at the same time – one closer, one some inches further away (to my right) and the last some inches further to my left.

Then I started to gain an answer to a question posed by my American friend; it is by allowing the beings 'into ourselves' that we can cooperate with them. This is also how we can help these beings to experience human and earthly existence.

The following day, the beings were halfway inside me. I felt a certain fear, but mainly excitement – or, rather, a more calm acceptance of their entering. I trusted that they did not want to take away my freedom and integrity. (Of course, all of us already have entities inside us.) Now I was cautious to observe any changes within myself. Would I simply become something of a servant or vehicle to them? Was this an exchange in which we helped each other, or was the help only going in one direction?

The next day, shortly before Easter, the three entities entered fully into my body. The dark reddish Vulcan being entered close to the area of the consciousness soul, thus helping especially against the azuric adversarial forces, as well as preparing for the future development of Atma.* The greenish-red Venus being entered close to the area of the intellectual soul, thus helping especially against the ahrimanic adversarial forces, as well as preparing for the future Buddhi. The yellowish-green Jupiter being entered close to the area of the sentient soul, thus helping against the luciferic adversarial forces, as well as preparing for the future Manas. (Again, this reminded me very much of my meeting with the hidden

---

*For the development of the human being's higher bodies, see Rudolf Steiner's *Theosophy*.

beings of Iceland, except that those elves did not intend primarily to help humans in the way that these other beings from the cosmos did.)

After all this 'entering', I felt quite exhausted, and the following night I slept for some eleven hours.

Over the following days, I had a certain tendency to a headache and colour-hallucinations. At one time, the whole room became full of flowing colours, and for a moment I was afraid that I was about to die from a stroke. I felt the presence of new soul contents and abilities. Both my arms and legs felt quite different, and my eyes experienced strange perceptions of different colours. For a while, this was all very odd...

*

Waking up the next morning, on Palm Sunday, I felt quite peculiar. Usually, when I wake up I feel like *myself*. Now, instead of *I*, I felt like *we*.

The next strange experience happened just after I had got up and was sitting as usual in front of our fireplace with my cup of morning coffee. The Vulcan being – the one that was human on the Saturn incarnation of the Earth – definitely liked the effect of the coffee, but the Venus being – the one that was human on the Sun incarnation of the Earth – definitely did not like the effect. He wrinkled his nose!

Later that evening, at my study group, we began with a short eurythmy exercise. All three beings were astonished, and did not really understand or like it.

The first actual information I received from them came two days later. This came especially from the Jupiter being – the one that had been human on the Moon development of the Earth, and who was supposed to

fulfil its development on the future Jupiter, our next
Earth incarnation. This information concerned the
connection between the moon, Vidar's mission and
why the presentation of Christ had to come from
the North – from Norway (Scandinavia) – towards
Europe. This was because the moon itself, actually
the quarter-moon or so-called sickle moon, was today
the grail of the new Christianity, the new revelation of
the Christ, or what Rudolf Steiner called the Northern
Grail.

To bring this revelation to Europe, the 'blood' of the
Grail had to be poured out onto the earth and the humans
living there. In the north, this outpouring was possible,
but going further south, it became less and less so. This
can easily be seen physically, as the sickle moon in the
south is more horizontal, and appears to pour out little, whilst, when travelling north, increasingly the sickle
moon appears to pour out content – onto the land and
people. I was surprised, as I never had thought about
this before.

After Easter, both Vidar, Balder and the Vulcans
were quiet. There was no communication at all, and I
became increasingly aware that liaising with the spiritual world was dependent on human beings posing
questions to this world. And, for the time being, I had
no questions.

*

Two weeks later, I received a question from a eurythmist living in Finland. My book on the teachings of
Vidar had been published for the first time in Finnish,
and was well received. Now this eurythmist wrote to
me, asking if I would ask Vidar about a problem she

had with eurythmy – about something she could not verbalize, but something she felt was 'missing'; in other words, something that needed to be added to the art of eurythmy.

I presented this question to Vidar on a Sunday afternoon, and on Monday morning some kind of answer started to take form. At first, this was an imagination of huge, dark streams of cotton, moving and flowing in space. That was on the first day.

The next day, this flowing of thick, cottonlike streams continued, but now in a more distinct way, as if the streams contained a meaning or communication. This went on through the whole of the second day. Still, though, I understood nothing of the meaning of this imagination. Then, on the third day, the meaning became clear in a precise way:

Eurythmy was constructed when humanity needed a development of the consciousness soul, and eurythmy was perfect for this. Today, humanity needs to strengthen the etheric body, especially as we are expected to experience Christ in the etheric. For this purpose, eurythmy needs to change. Such a change could bring etheric movements, as represented in the imagination of movements of thick, swirling cotton.

The next day, early in the morning, I received the following teaching from Vidar. The sum of these insights was as follows:

- Eurythmy is a method that can stimulate or develop several aspects of the human body and/ or the world itself. This includes the consciousness soul, the other soul aspects, the etheric body and/or the astral body – all depending on what the practitioner wants to do and has the

knowledge to do. It can thus be used to strengthen
the consciousness-soul, or it can also be used to
work more directly into the etheric body.

- When used to heal and/or stimulate the Earth
  or animals, eurythmy in its usual form can stimulate or develop the part of the animal/plant
  that is connected to human consciousness. It
  thus gives the animal/plant a mixture of human
  forces, both beneficial and malignant.
- Eurythmy can also be used to stimulate or
  develop the etheric body of the animal/plant
  directly, but then it should not go through the
  human being itself, but directly to the animal/
  plant. Otherwise, other movements should be
  used.

*

The next question I received was from a friend in Järna,
Sweden – a locality that comprises the centre of the
anthroposophic movement in Sweden. Was Järna sufficiently spiritual to be able to support the new Christ
revelation brought about through Vidar? The answer to
this question also took three days to arrive. Vidar said
that the area was sufficiently light-filled, but the main
house – presumably referring to the anthroposophical
centre – was too dark, at least right now. That was a succinct and quick response.

I came to realize that there were two ways to ask a
question to Vidar: I could ask a succinct, specific question myself, or I could ask a more complex question
from another person. If the question was either simple
or came from myself, the answer would be immedi-
ate and brief. If the question either came from another

human being or was in essence complicated, the answer usually took three days, or even double that.

*

The next question – and the last I will present here – was from one of the translators of the Finnish edition of my book. Could Vidar elaborate on the fourth part of the soul, the part that Vidar called 'time-karma-Christ'. What really is time?

The answer began with an imagination, which took two days. It showed clouds – masses of clouds. Not like those in the outer etheric realm, but puffy, cumulus clouds, like those here in our world. The second day, the masses of white cumulus clouds changed into stone, like smooth granite – rather like the rocks one can see on the coastline of Norway, polished by water, ice, sea and storms. There were three main rocks in the imagination.

The third day the explanation arrived, with overwhelming emphasis and strength. This was received as an intuition, and indicated that time originated in the clouds of the outer etheric realm. From these clouds, time then gradually materialized and hardened, becoming more and more material throughout history. Time remains as three 'streams', however. Then, at a certain point, this hardening of time turned.

This turning-point is what Rudolf Steiner referred to as the 'Turning-point of Time'. This was the year 33, the Mystery of Golgotha, when the three streams of time turned from a downward and hardening path to an upwards and spiritualizing one. This path will and must be our path back to the outer etheric, where Christ can be found, and through which the three elemental realms can be transformed and Christianized.

The three streams of time also relate to the three elemental realms: one stream from the future, one from the past and one in the present. The third realm, relating to Lucifer, comes from the future. The second realm, relating to Ahriman, comes from the past. And the first realm is the present, where both Christ and the Azuras may be found.

Vidar then also revealed a further secret of our soul aspects, namely thinking, feeling and will. These, too, originate in the outer etheric world, in the forces or parts of this world that are purely spiritual. Feeling comes from the *waters* of this world, thinking from the *winds*, whilst the will comes from *solid ground*. All these parts of the outer etheric world are mirrored or reflected in the human soul, thus creating soul abilities or faculties that, with time, we can spiritualize and make our own: *spiritual thinking*, *spiritual feeling* and *spiritual will* – plus spiritual 'time-Christ-karma', for which as yet we have no proper name.

This knowledge also helped made sense of my earlier observation from some 30 years ago. Then, I had discovered that, by stepping into the etheric streams that occur between trees, I could travel in time. As described in several of my earlier books, I can travel to the past by entering the etheric streams by moving to the left, luciferic side of my body. By moving to the right, ahrimanic side of my body, I can travel to the future.

These etheric streams between the trees are closely related to the clouds of the outer etheric world, where, I now understand, lies the origin of time. The three time streams are thus also related to the luciferic, ahrimanic and Christ-forces (as well as the azuric forces), which thus give us the illusion of physical existence. Time is part of that illusion, but in origin highly spiritual – as the clouds of the outer etheric are also the medium through which Christ will reappear (in the etheric realm). As such, then, the fourth aspect of our soul is called by Vidar, 'time-Christ-karma'.

*

A few hours later, a further teaching on time entered my soul, and to understand this we should recapitulate the concept of the soul. The soul has up until recently consisted of thinking, feeling and will. Thus, the spiritual understanding of different matters has consisted of imagination, inspiration and intuition – imagination being the understanding in thinking, in the spiritual part of the etheric body, which also is described as the intellectual soul, the precursor of the Life Spirit or Buddhi.

Further, inspiration is the understanding in the feeling, in the spiritual part of the astral body, which also is described as the sentient soul, the precursor of Spirit Self or Manas. Finally, intuition is the understanding in the will, in the spiritual part of the physical body, or the 'I'-organization, which also is described as the consciousness soul, the precursor of Spirit Man or Atma.

Now, if there is a fourth part of the soul that is being developed, a part that Vidar called or described as 'time-Christ-karma', then there must be a fourth level of cognition or understanding, a level of pure experience – of not 'seeing' as in imagination, of not 'communicating' as in inspiration, and of not being 'inside or at one with' the spiritual being or aspect of reality as in intuition— but 'living or experiencing' the understanding. This level may need a new word (if it doesn't exist already) – something like *Inexperiation*!?

Well, after some hours I reached this level. I experienced the switching of time and space. I was almost certain that I was dying, but I didn't die. Later, I thought that perhaps time and space are switched after death – so it was not so strange that I thought I was going to die.

Through this process, I understood that Vidar, the servant of the Living Christ, brought insights and information on the path we should take to reach Christ. Also, that today this path is in some ways connected to Norway, as Vidar is closely connected to that part of Scandinavia.

I also understood that the cosmic wisdom had its servant in Sophia, the Archangel of the Slavic people, who will also later become an Archai.

Sophia is the cosmic intelligence or wisdom, which is above the spiritual hierarchies. Whichever spiritual being mediates this wisdom might be referred to as Sophia. As this wisdom is now destined to be channelled through the sixth cultural epoch – the future Slavic or Russian epoch, which will follow our present, fifth one – we could speak of the Slavic folk soul as being penetrated by cosmic wisdom or Sophia.

Thus, Christ – the Way the Truth and the Life – and Sophia – the divine Wisdom – support their servants, Michael and Vidar.

*

At this point, I would like to end these observations, reflections and reports of my current research. I thank you for bearing with me and sharing these thoughts and ideas, many of which are still in the process of 'becoming'. I would like to remind the reader that the contents of this book are not intended as fixed teachings, new dogmas or beliefs, but are brought forth in the spirit of collegial scientific investigation and discovery.

A note from the publisher

For more than a quarter of a century, **Temple Lodge Publishing** has made available new thought, ideas and research in the field of spiritual science.

Anthroposophy, as founded by Rudolf Steiner (1861-1925), is commonly known today through its practical applications, principally in education (Steiner-Waldorf schools) and agriculture (biodynamic food and wine). But behind this outer activity stands the core discipline of spiritual science, which continues to be developed and updated. True science can never be static and anthroposophy is living knowledge.

Our list features some of the best contemporary spiritual-scientific work available today, as well as introductory titles. So, visit us online at **www.templelodge.com** and join our emailing list for news on new titles.

If you feel like supporting our work, you can do so by buying our books or making a direct donation (we are a non-profit/ charitable organisation).

office@templelodge.com

For the finest books of Science and Spirit